Numerical Methods using MATLAB

Abhishek K Gupta

Apress®

Numerical Methods using MATLAB

ISBN-13 (pbk): 978-1-4842-0155-8

ISBN-13 (electronic): 978-1-4842-0154-1

Managing Director: Welmoed Spahr
Lead Editor: Ewan Buckingham
Technical Reviewer: Shubham Tomar
Editorial Board: Steve Anglin, Mark Beckner, Gary Cornell, Louise Corrigan, Jim DeWolf, Jonathan Gennick, Robert Hutchinson, Michelle Lowman, James Markham, Matthew Moodie, Jeff Olson, Jeffrey Pepper, Douglas Pundick, Ben Renow-Clarke, Gwenan Spearing, Steve Weiss
Coordinating Editor: Jill Balzano
Copy Editor: Barnaby Sheppard
Compositor: SPi Global
Indexer: SPi Global
Artist: SPi Global
Cover Designer: Anna Ishchenko

Distributed to the book trade worldwide by Springer Science+Business Media New York, 233 Spring Street, 6th Floor, New York, NY 10013. Phone 1-800-SPRINGER, fax (201) 348-4505, e-mail orders-ny@springer-sbm.com, or visit www.springeronline.com. Apress Media, LLC is a California LLC and the sole member (owner) is Springer Science + Business Media Finance Inc (SSBM Finance Inc). SSBM Finance Inc is a Delaware corporation.

For information on translations, please e-mail rights@apress.com, or visit www.apress.com.

Apress and friends of ED books may be purchased in bulk for academic, corporate, or promotional use. eBook versions and licenses are also available for most titles. For more information, reference our Special Bulk Sales–eBook Licensing web page at www.apress.com/bulk-sales.

Any source code or other supplementary material referenced by the author in this text is available to readers at www.apress.com. For detailed information about how to locate your book's source code, go to www.apress.com/source-code/.

Dedicated to My Parents
Shri Basant Prasad & Smt Damayanti Gupta

Contents at a Glance

Contents

About the Author

Abhishek K Gupta received his B.Tech. and M.Tech. degrees in Electrical Engineering from IIT Kanpur, India, in 2010. He is currently a Ph.D. student at The University of Texas at Austin, where his research has focused on stochastic geometry and its applications in wireless communication. His other research interests include multiuser MIMO systems and optimization. He was a recipient of a GE-FS Leadership Award from the General Electric (GE) Foundation and the Institute of International Education in 2009. He is also the author of the book MATLAB by Examples (2010) and a blog with the same name. He has been teaching MATLAB and its applications in engineering for many years.

Acknowledgments

I want to give my sincere thanks to Shruti Desai who helped me in revising this book and reporting errors by carefully reviewing the complete manuscript and providing me with constructive feedback. I want to express my deep acknowledgement to Dr Shaun A Forth for introducing me to MATLAB.

I am very thankful to the entire editing team at Apress Media for their continuous support and patience and for making this book a reality while keeping the whole writing experience smooth and enjoyable. I am thankful to my friends Somsubhra Barik and Harpreet Singh for giving me constant support at all times. Lastly, I want to express my gratitude to God, my parents, my sisters Rashmi, Gunjan and Sonali and their significant others who have been with me at every moment of my life.

Introduction

I had my first experience with MATLAB in my second year of engineering while working on control systems design. Later on, in my internship, I got an opportunity to develop a package named MAD in MATLAB under Dr Shaun A Forth at DCMT, UK. From there on, my interest in MATLAB kept on increasing. The journey thus started never stopped and MATLAB has become an inseparable component of my research life. I have become a big fan of MATLAB due to its simplicity and its vectorization capability. I enjoy programming in MATLAB. This book is my attempt to make others a fan of it too.

This book presents a wide range of numerical methods and their implementation in MATLAB with the help of examples to make the learning more interactive. A conventional method to teach numerical methods is to first give a detailed discussion of such methods and then present a few examples. This method is very far from being efficient and by the time the actual implementation comes, the user who is mainly interested in solving his own problems has already given up. This book takes a very different approach by stressing the concept of trying out techniques by oneself, and attempts to start the discussion with examples long before the actual theory is introduced. The idea behind the book came to me when I taught a course on MATLAB to a small batch of students at my home institution. During the course, I had encountered the problems which students face while learning it. As a student and researcher I understand what a researcher or student looks for in a book and hence I believe this book will prove to be valuable to the intended audience. Instead of bombarding users with theory and information, the book only gives concise and practical information to help you to effectively solve your research problem in less time.

This book presents each and every topic in a very concise and readable format which helps you to learn quickly and effectively. This book can also serve as a complementary book for a MATLAB course in engineering colleges. Also, it is designed to be a companion in your research anywhere you go. This book assumes that the user has a basic knowledge of MATLAB programming and quickly covers the MATLAB basics in the first chapter. If the user is not familiar with MATLAB, he should read some basic MATLAB books prior to starting this book. One such book is written by me and titled "MATLAB by Examples", published by Finch Publications (2010).

This book is divided into 10 chapters. The first two chapters are written to help users to quickly understand MATLAB. Chapter 1 covers the basic programming paradigm of MATLAB, including how to write functions, scripts and data structures. Chapter 2 quickly covers one of the most important features of MATLAB known as vectorization, which will help you to write efficient programs in MATLAB.

The third chapter is probably the most important chapter and provides the foundation of the book. It covers all the important operations basic to any numerical computation. Once the user is familiar with these fundamental operations and learns how to implement them, the rest of the book should come naturally to him.

The fourth chapter provides a quick tutorial for visualizing any output and results in MATLAB using simple plots and animations.

The fifth chapter discusses the primary concepts and methodology behind any numerical simulation. It talks about how we can solve any numerical computations using MATLAB and presents some key examples to elaborate on the topics more clearly. Building on the fifth chapter, the sixth chapter incorporates random components in any system or simulation and introduces the idea behind Monte Carlo simulations.

Chapter 7 acquaints you with the powerful tool of optimization in MATLAB. Since MATLAB provides a wide range of inbuilt functions to solve any optimization problem, this chapter gives a comprehensive review of all the important methods. However, learning to implement such methods from scratch is also crucial to developing a proper understanding and approach towards numerical methods. The chapter also elaborates on the paradigm behind the full implementation of such methods with examples. Building on this, Chapter 8 presents a brief but complete description of evolutionary algorithms such as the genetic algorithm and swarm intelligence algorithms, e.g. particle swarm optimization.

Chapter 9 is written for data scientists and statisticians. Regression and model fitting play an important role in all modern era applications, be it time-series analysis or market prediction in the financial domain or the recommender system in online economics. This chapter covers the main approach behind regression with an appropriate amount of theory to provide an optimal reading and learning experience for the users.

Chapter 10 is written for control system engineers and researchers interested in understanding the dynamics of any system. It is built on Chapters 5 and 6 and, using tools from these two chapters and inbuilt functions, it provides a concise yet detailed overview of simulating the dynamics and time evolution of real world continuous and discrete systems.

CHAPTER 1

■ ■ ■

Introduction to MATLAB

In this chapter, we will talk about the basics of MATLAB and how to get started with it. We expect the reader to have basic programming skills, and therefore we will not cover any MATLAB programming concepts in detail. When discussing any topic, we will try not to go into such specifics that cause us to deviate from our main goal. Instead, we will provide proper references which can be consulted for more information.

Introduction

MATLAB is a programming language created with the basic goal of providing a simple intuitive platform for engineering design applications. However, as well as being a programming language, it can also be classified as software for computation and visualization. On one hand, you can call sophisticated programming routines in MATLAB, while on the other hand you can just open a simple graphical user interface to fill in the specifications, click OK, and MATLAB will perform computations and visualize it for you.

As we will see in later chapters, most engineering tasks require processing of matrices, for example image processing or data regression. MATLAB provides an excellent platform and routines for matrix operations. In fact, MATLAB is short for MATrix LABoratory because its main feature is to provide direct operations on matrices and to avoid complicated loops.

Current engineering applications use numerical simulations extensively, which require specific functions along with a programming language. For example, a signal processing application will need filter, fft and similar basic functions. In typical programming environments such as C/C++, you need to write these basic functions yourself. MATLAB provides all such basic and advanced functions in built-in packages known as toolboxes. MATLAB currently has a wide range of toolboxes for different engineering fields, *e.g.* it has toolboxes devoted to signal processing, image processing, communication, control systems and finance. In addition, some engineers are more inclined towards graphical models and want to avoid writing programming routines. MATLAB also features Simulink, which provides a platform for building and simulating graphical models without knowledge of programming.

MATLAB provides an interactive environment to perform engineering tasks for most current fields. You can also use your own toolboxes or use extra toolboxes built by others, which are freely available at the MATLAB File exchange at the following address:

http://http://www.mathworks.com/matlabcentral/fileexchange.

With its intuitive language, minimalistic programming commands, capability of one shot matrix operations, a wide range of toolboxes for most engineering fields, interactive platform and excellent visualization capabilities, MATLAB is regarded as an excellent and preferred tool for academic research and industrial applications.

Interface

After you have successfully installed MATLAB, you can open it by double clicking the icon or typing `matlab` in the terminal/run window. Depending on your machine, you will see something like Figure 1-1. The whole interface is known as the MATLAB Desktop. It consists of many components and windows which can be reorganized and enabled/disabled by mouse actions or via Desktop ➤ Layout menu options. Here are some of the important components one can find in a standard MATLAB Desktop:

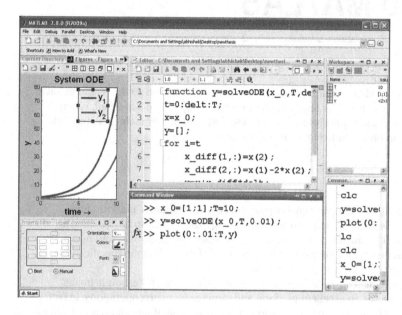

Figure 1-1. *MATLAB Desktop*

Command Window

The command window can be considered as a terminal. It is shown at the bottom of the middle column in Figure 1-1. Here, you can type your commands and run MATLAB programs (known as scripts). MATLAB displays >> as the command prompt.

Current Directory

The Current Directory in MATLAB represents a directory in which MATLAB looks for the functions and program files. In order to run a program, it must be in the current directory. The Current Directory window shows all the files and folders in the current directory. You can change the current directory or even add some folders to the MATLAB search path.

Workspace

The MATLAB workspace contains all the variables present and is shown at the top right of Figure 1-1. MATLAB programming differs from conventional programming languages in the sense that any variables created during a program execution remain, even after the program has executed, until you explicitly clear them or close the MATLAB session.

Figures

MATLAB uses figure windows to display any plot or visualization. This is shown in the leftmost column of Figure 1-1. We can open multiple figure windows using the figure command.

Command History

The command history window stores and displays all previous MATLAB commands issued in the command window. You can rerun any command by double clicking on the command window. We can also access the command via the keyboard, using the up and down arrow keys.

Editor

MATLAB provides an integrated editor to write commands and programs and execute them. The editor also can be used to debug programs. It is shown at the top middle of Figure 1-1.

Help Browser

MATLAB provides excellent documentation for all its functions with sufficient examples. To open MATLAB help, you can type doc or go to Help ➤ Product Help. To directly open help about a function (for example sin), we would type

```
doc sin;
```

Getting Started

In our first example, we will create a simple program to multiply two numbers. MATLAB programs are called scripts or also M-files because their extension is '.m'. To create a script named myfirstprogram.m, let us go to the command window and type

```
edit myfirstprogram
```

MATLAB will open an editor window with a blank file name. Type the following code

```
a=4;
b=3;
c=a*b;
disp(c);
```

Save this file and run the code by entering the following in the command window

```
myfirstprogram
```

When you press enter, you get the following output

```
c=
   12
```

Let us spend some time in understanding this simple program. We don't need any sophisticated program definitions or imports to run a simple program such as multiplication in MATLAB. In this program, we have defined two variables a and b. To define/assign a variable, we simply need to type

```
variablename= variablevalue;
```

We then multiplied them to store the answer in c and displayed it using the disp command.

The semicolon used to terminate each line is not necessary. If the semicolon is omitted, MATLAB will also display the value computed in the right-hand side of the statement. For example, typing

```
c=a*b;
```

will result in the computation of c without displaying the result, while typing

```
c=a*b
```

will result in the computation of c and also result in the display of the output in the command window. We can change the value of any variable by reassigning its value. For example

```
c=7;
```

will change the value of c to 7.

The first question which comes to our mind concerns the type of a. Is it stored as a double or an integer? First of all, all the variables stored in MATLAB are matrices. Secondly, all the numerical values are treated as double. So 4 is a 1×1 double numerical matrix. So if we compute the division of a by b using

```
c=a/b
```

we will get 1.33. However, the thing to remember is that even if a is a double number, MATLAB still knows that it can also be treated as an integer. This will be better understood in later chapters, when we try to index the matrix by providing integer indices.

Creating a Matrix

To create a matrix, we enclose all the elements inside [ ]. For example, to create a row vector containing the six elements 1 3 5 6 3 2, we can write

```
A= [1 3 5 6 3 2]
```

or

```
A=[1,3,5,6,3,2]
```

The comma or space here separates the elements into a single row and instructs MATLAB to construct a new column for the next element. Similarly we can construct a column vector with the same elements by typing

```
A=[1;3;5;6;3;2]
```

Here, each semicolon tells MATLAB to start a new row for the next element. Both comma and semicolon operators can also be used to join two matrices, for example

```
A=[4;5];
C=[2;A];
```

or

```
C=[2; [4;5]]
```

We can also mix these two operators to form a rectangular matrix.

```
A=[2 3 ; 4 5 ; 6 7]
B=[[2;4;6] , [3 ;5;7]]
C=[2 [3] ; [4;6] [5 7]]
```

All three of the above operations give the same 3×2 matrix. There is another operator ':', known as the colon operator, which means 'to'. For example, to create a matrix with elements from 0 to 100 with unit difference, we can type

```
A=[0:100];
```

To create a matrix with elements from 0 to 2π with step 0.01, we type

```
t=[0:.01:2*pi]
```

which can be interpreted as 'from 0 to 2*pi with step .01'. Remember that pi is a pre-defined constant in MATLAB.

Now you can write these commands in the editor window and save/run it as an M-file. But you can also type these commands directly into the command window. As we press enter after each command, that command will be executed and the result will be the same as if it were executed as a script in the editor window. The benefit of writing the commands in a script file is that it can be saved for future use, and it can be transferred among devices. However, the command window can be used to test or view variables quickly. There are some cases where we want to run a small command over some variables and we know that we will never use this command in the near future. In those cases, an M-file is not needed and the command window can be used instead.

Functions

A function is a simple set of instructions which accepts some inputs and returns outputs. There are a wide range of inbuilt functions in MATLAB for different application and they can be called anywhere with proper inputs. A function call generally has the following syntax

```
[output1 output2]= functionname (input1, input2)
```

Consider the function sin which takes a vector and computes the sine of each of its elements, returning a vector consisting of the values in the same order as the input. To view the syntax of the sin function we can type:

```
help sin
```

which displays a short description of the sin function and its syntax with some examples.

```
Sin:
Sine of argument in radians
Syntax
Y = sin(X)
Description
Y = sin(X) returns the circular sine of the elements of X. The sin function operates element-wise on
arrays. The function's domains and ranges include complex values. All angles are in radians.
```

After reading this, we can easily guess the format of the sin function. Now we can use this function as follows:

```
x=0:.01:2*pi;
y=sin(x);
```

Similarly, there is a wide range of functions such as log, exp, etc., which can be found at http://www.mathworks.com/help/matlab/functionlist.html. We will encounter many of these functions as we go. Two of the most interesting features of MATLAB are that these functions have very intuitive names and syntax, and their syntax can be easily found just by going to MATLAB help.

In MATLAB, we can also define our own functions. Suppose we want to define a function myfun which computes y=log(x)*sin(x/4) given the input x. We first create an M-file by typing

```
edit myfun
```

and then we type the following

```
function y= myfun(x)
y=log(x)*sin(x/4);
```

saving it to a file. Such a file is called a function file and has the same extension .m as a script. The first word of the first line of this code tells MATLAB that it is a function file. Everything before the equals sign tells MATLAB what variables to output and the word immediately after the equals sign is the function name by which MATLAB remembers this function. This name should match the name of the file. The name is followed by a list of all the input parameters inside parentheses. The rest of the code contains instructions to compute output variables from input variables.

To call this function, we write

```
x1 = 5
y=myfun(x1);
```

in any script, function or command window. Similarly, we can define a multiple input and output functions as

```
function [z p]= myfun(x,y)
z=log(x)*sin(y/4);
p=exp(x)*cos(z/4);
```

and this function can be called by

```
[a1 b1]=myfun(x,2);
```

If a function has no inputs, you can call this function by

```
out=myfunction()
```

or

```
out=myfunction
```

The Difference Between Functions and Scripts

Functions and scripts are both M-files, but there are a few differences between them. As we saw, the first line defines whether the M-file is a function or a script. A function has a particular set of inputs and outputs, while a script doesn't. A script can use all the variables created in the MATLAB workspace, but a function can only use the variables specially passed to it. After the execution is over, a script returns all the variables to the workspace while a function only returns the variables listed as outputs and deletes the rest of the variables. Scripts use the same copy of a variable in the MATLAB workspace and modifying any variable in any script will affect the original copy in the workspace while a function creates a new copy of all the variables when they are called and any modification to these variables doesn't affect the original variables. In other words, when a function is called from a workspace, the function call creates a new workspace, copies variables to it, computes outputs and returns these variables to the calling workspace, deleting its own workspace. You can also call a script from a function. In that case, the script will use the calling function's workspace and the variables created by this script call will also get deleted when the calling function finishes its execution.

As we saw, scripts, variables and functions (with no input) are called in the same way. For example, to display a variable finalsum we write

```
finalsum
```

and to run a script named scrfinal we write

```
scrfinal
```

Similarly, to multiply the variable finalsum by 2, we write

```
x=2*finalsum;
```

and if there is a function named mypiconst defined as

```
function x=mypiconst
x=3.14;
```

we can multiply the output of this function by 2 by writing

```
x=2*mypiconst;
```

What if there is a variable named finalsum and a script file with name finalsum.m? How does MATLAB know which one to use? The answer is that MATLAB first searches for the variable in its workspace and if it cannot find any matching variable then it searches for scripts or functions in the current directory. In other words, a variable shadows a script or function with the same name. This is also true for inbuilt functions. For example, we saw that sin is used to compute the sine of a variable. Let us define our own variable sin and then try to call the sin function

```
sin=4;
d=sin*3
y=sin(3);
```

We will get d=12, but the next line will cause an error because sin is treated as a variable here and it is trying to access the third element of the sin matrix. Here, (.) denotes indexing, which we will learn more about later. To see this explicitly, we can ask MATLAB about any variable name/function to determine which version MATLAB is using by typing

```
which sin
```

to which MATLAB displays

```
sin is variable.
```

To use the function sin again, we need to delete the sin variable first by typing

```
clear sin
```

To clear all the variables, we type

```
clear all
```

Now typing which sin results in

```
sin is inbuilt function.
```

This is crucial and we need to remember it, otherwise we would constantly run into errors or unexpected outputs. For example, in the above code, if we use

```
sin=4;
d=sin*3
y=sin(1);
```

it will run without error because y will be assigned the first element of the sin variable, which is 4. So instead of getting 0.8414, you will get y=4, and all subsequent computations will be incorrect, possibly without us realizing the mistake.

Special Matrices

We can also create some special matrices via inbuilt functions. For example, to create matrix of size 5×6 all entries of which are ones, we can write

```
A=ones(5,6);
```

Similarly zeros will create an all zero matrix, eye will create an identity matrix and rand will create a matrix whose entries are random values between 0 and 1.

Other Variable Types

We saw that MATLAB creates variables of type matrix. Until now, we have only seen variables containing numerical matrix values. In this section, we will meet a few other types of variables that MATLAB implements.

Character Variables

A character variable is a string containing characters. Remember that a single character is just a 1×1 character matrix. To define a string we write

```
A='strval';
```

which is equivalent to

```
A=['s' 't' 'r' 'v' 'a' 'l'];
```

To define multiline strings, we need to define each row with the same number of columns by including spaces. For example

```
A=['john';'joe'];
```

Cells

When a collection contains elements of different types, they can be represented using a cell array. A multiline string can be better represented using cells since different elements in a cell can have a different number of columns, hence strings with different lengths.

```
A={'name', 12};
A={'john','joe'};
```

Logical Variables

Logical or boolean variables can have only two values, true (1) or false (0). To create a logical matrix, we write

```
A=[true, false, true];
```

or

```
A=logical([1,0,1]);
```

Structures

A structure has many variables attached to it, indexed by fields. For example, a student is attached to variables declaring his name, class and cgpa. To construct a student structure, we write

```
student.name='John';
student.class=10;
student.cgpa=3.5;
```

which results in a structure matrix of size 1×1. To create a second element of the above matrix, we can write

```
student(2).name='Joe';
student(2).class=9;
student(2).cgpa=3.7;
```

Saving/Loading Variables

Since MATLAB deletes all its variables when it is closed, you can save all the variables in a data file for the next session by executing the following

```
save filename
```

Similarly we can load all the variables using

```
load filename
```

Plots

MATLAB also provides easy and simple plotting functions. To plot data, you need two vectors of the same size, one for the x axis and the other for the y axis. When we call plot with these two vectors, MATLAB will create a pair (x,y) by taking corresponding elements from these two vectors, plotting them on a Cartesian plane and connecting them by straight lines.

The following example shows how to plot a rectangle in MATLAB (see Figure 1-2)

```
x=[1 0 -1 0 1];
y=[0 1 0 -1 0];
plot(x,y);
```

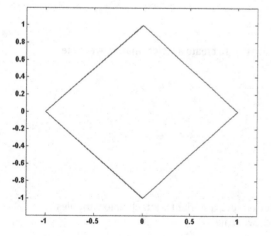

Figure 1-2. *Plotting a rectangle*

If the x values are very close to one another, the plot will look like a continuous plot (See Figure 1-3)

```
t=0:.01:2*pi;
y=sin(t);
plot(t,y);
```

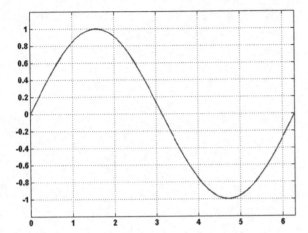

Figure 1-3. *Plotting a continuous function*

In later sections we will see other plotting functions in greater detail.

▪ ▪ ▪

CHAPTER 2

Matrix Representation, Operations and Vectorization

Recall that MATLAB is an abbreviation for Matrix Laboratory. Everything in MATLAB is a matrix, be it a scalar, variable or an image. The primary motivation behind building an entire piece of software for matrices was the fact that matrices are very important in engineering. Almost everyone has seen matrices in mathematics, where they are used for linear transformations, but matrices are also used in a wide range of applications in engineering where they represent a variety of different notions. In this section, we will see different representations of matrices, their applications, and learn different operations on them. Another important aspect is the trick known as vectorization. Since we will be dealing with big matrices, we will see that it is important to avoid loops over matrices using this trick.

Matrix Representation

In this section, we'll look at ways to represent matrices.

Conventional Sense: Matrices

Matrices are widely used in mathematics, especially in Linear Algebra. Recall that a matrix is a two-dimensional set of elements. The most common usage is to represent a transformation on some space. For example, consider a 2D vector

$$x = \begin{bmatrix} 2 \\ 3 \end{bmatrix}.$$

Let us take the rotation matrix A as

$$A = \begin{bmatrix} 0 & 1 \\ -1 & 0 \end{bmatrix}.$$

Now define y as

$$y = Ax = \begin{bmatrix} 0 & 1 \\ -1 & 0 \end{bmatrix} \begin{bmatrix} 2 \\ 3 \end{bmatrix} = \begin{bmatrix} 3 \\ -2 \end{bmatrix}$$

which is the $90°$ rotated version of x.

Data Sense: Arrays

There is a whole new meaning of matrices in engineering where they can also be used to represent data. Such matrices are called arrays. For example, consider an input signal to an electric motor shown in Figure 2-1.

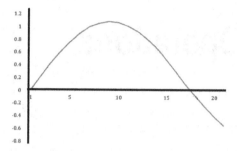

Figure 2-1. *Input signal to an electric motor*

The same signal can be represented as the following matrix:

```
x=[0.0048 0.21 0.41 0.597 0.76 0.89 1.00 1.059 1.085 1.07 1.01 0.92 0.80 0.65 0.48 0.29 0.10
-0.0773565 -0.25 -0.41 -0.55];
```

An image is another example of such data representation. A color image is a three dimensional matrix. For example, the small 4×4 pixel image in Figure 2-2 can be represented as the following matrix

```
A=[1 2 0 2;3 2 1 3;3 2 1 0;1 3 2 2];
```

where 0 1 2 3 denotes black, red, green and blue respectively.

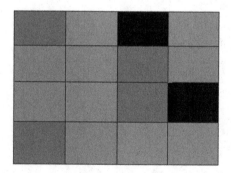

Figure 2-2. *A sample image*

A set of points representing a plot is another example of such a representation.

Model Representation

In engineering, we often model a physical system as a mathematical model where each such model consists of some parameters and design equations. These parameters can also be represented as matrices. The simplest example is a polynomial. Consider $p(x) = x^3 - 2x^2 + 6x + 4$. We can represent this as the matrix p=[3 -2 6 4]. Other examples are neural networks, transfer functions etc. Consider the transfer function

$$F(s) = \frac{s+3}{s^2 + 3s + 2}$$

which is a ratio of two polynomials, so we can represent it by two vectors n1=[1 3] and d=[1 3 2]. How we are going to use these vectors for model computations (for example, step response) is something we need to remember. Note that all these representations look the same. Since they are represented as matrices, there is no distinction between them from the perspective of MATLAB. When storing some p, MATLAB doesn't make any distinction as to whether p denotes a polynomial or a neural network's bias value. The programmer needs to remember what a vector/matrix represents.

Operations

MATLAB provides a wide range of operations and functions you can perform over vectors. In MATLAB, you can represent each operator as a function too. Therefore, in this discussion, we will be using functions and operators interchangeably. Since a matrix can represent various different notions, as we have seen in the previous section, there are different functions/operators suited for different representations, sometimes with almost the same name and/or purpose. This section will describe these operations and their important differences.

Matrix Operations

The operators that are performed over matrices in their conventional mathematical sense and which follow the laws of linear algebra are known as matrix operators. For example, to invert a transformation, we can use the invert operator or pinv function.

If $y = Ax$ then $x = A^*y$, where A^* is the Moore-Penrose inverse, which can be computed as follows:

```
x=[2 3 5];
A=[1 0 -1;1 1 0;1 2 3];
y=Ax;
x=pinv(A)*y
```

Suppose we apply a transformation operator twice:

```
y=A*A*x;
```

This is equivalent to computing the square of a matrix via the matrix power operator

```
Asq=A^2
```

and computing y by

```
y=Asq*x
```

Similarly you can compute the square root either by calling the function

```
y=sqrtm(A)*x
```

or via the power operator as

```
y=A^0.5*x
```

We can also compute the product of two matrices using the function mtimes or the * operator

```
B=mtimes(A,C);
B=A*C;
```

Both of the above lines return the same results. Remember that this is matrix multiplication according to the rules of linear algebra, so the number of columns in A should match the number of rows in C, otherwise the multiplication is not defined and MATLAB will return an error.

Note the letter m in sqrtm and mtimes, which denotes 'matrix'. Since the square root and multiplication operations are defined differently for different representations of matrices, the matrix versions are sqrtm and mtimes. The former computes the matrix square root in the convention mathematical sense. Other important operations are +, \ (mldivide), / (mrdivide), '(ctranspose), ^ (mpower). Readers can refer to the MATLAB documentation for a full list of operations at http://www.mathworks.com/help/matlab/matlab_prog/array-vs-matrix-operations.html. There are also some operators which can only be used in this representation, such as eigenvalue and determinant, which can be computed using the following commands

```
y=eig(A);
z=det(A);
```

Dot (array) Operators

Recall that matrices can also represent data and each element of such a matrix denotes a data value (e.g. time sampled data point, field value at a spatial point). When we perform an operation on such a matrix, it means that we are performing the same operation at each element independently. Such an elementwise operation is known as a dot operation or array operation and this type of operation must be used for data matrices. For example, consider a matrix V containing voltage values at time [0:0.1:1] given as

```
V=[0  .19  .38  .56  .71  .84  .93  .98  .99  .97  .90];
```

and the matrix I representing current values at the same time instances, given as

```
I=[.29  .47  .64  .78  .89  .96  .99  .99  .94  .86  .74];
```

Now we can compute the power values at each time instant by

```
P=V.*I
```

The .* operator is known as the times operator and is used to multiply two matrices elementwise. Compare the times operator with the mtimes operator discussed in the previous section. The letter 'm' is used to differentiate between the two types of multiplication. Here, the times operator is only valid if either the two matrices have the same size or if at least one of them is a scalar. Note that if one of the matrices is a scalar, the times and mtimes operators result in the same operation.

Unlike matrix operators, array operators support multi-dimension matrices and operations other than arithmetic operations. We discuss some of these operators here:

Arithmetic Operators

Most arithmetic operators are the array (elementwise) versions of matrix operations and result in numerical values. For example, +, -, .*, ./ (rdivide), .\ (ldivide), transpose (.') , power (.^) are used to add, subtract, multiply, divide, left divide, transpose or compute powers of matrices. Most of these operators support scalar matrices or when one of the operands is a scalar. For example,

```
A=3;
B=[2 3; 4 5];
C=[1 2; 3 4];
G=B.^A
```

will result in

```
G=[8 27;64 125]
```

while

```
G=B.^C
```

will pair each corresponding elements $(B(i), C(i))$ in B and C for each i and compute $B(i) \wedge C(i)$, placing them at the ith position in G to give

```
G=[2 9;64 625]
```

Other arithmetic operators are trigonometric, exponential, and logarithmic operators. For example, assume X=[1 4 5]. To compute $y(x) = x^2 + e^{0.4x} + \sin(x)\log(x)$ for each of the elements of X, we can write

```
Y=X.^2+exp(.4.*X)+log(x).*sin(X).
```

Note that since 0.4 is a scalar, we will occasionally use * instead of .*, keeping in the mind that * in fact represents the array operation and is being used only because it gives the same result as .*. For example, the following is equivalent to the previous computation

```
Y=X.^2+exp(.4*X)+log(x).*sin(X).
```

Note that since addition and subtraction are elementwise in both the matrix and array sense, there is no separate matrix and dot version of + and -.

There are other arithmetic operators which work on the matrix as a whole (which makes sense only for data representation) such as sum. The following example computes the average velocity of a system from a vector V containing the instantaneous velocities of it at uniform time samples:

```
avgV=sum(V)/length(V)
```

Note that since sum(V) and length(V) are both scalars, using the ./ and / operators result in the same answer, therefore we can use / here. Other similar operations are prod, mean, etc. Note that for higher dimensional matrices, these operations can be done in any dimension which results in different outputs. For example, consider the matrix

```
A=[2 3 5;1 2 4];
```

Note that the first dimension in MATLAB is taken to be the column dimension. Therefore the function sum will result in the columnwise sum

```
s=sum(A)
```

giving

```
s=[3 5 9].
```

However, if we need the operation to be performed in a different dimension, we can specify it. For example, the following will result in the rowwise sum

```
s=sum(A,2)
```

giving

```
s=[ 10
     7 ];
```

The operation cumsum computes the cumulative sum of any vector/matrix. Suppose (x, p) denotes the probability mass function of a random variable X

```
x=[0 2 5 7 10];
p=[.2 .4 .1 .05 .25];
```

We can compute the cumulative distribution function (cdf) by the following

```
f1=cumsum(p);
f=[.2 f1]
```

Note the use of appending the element 0.2 in f. Since cumsum's output f1 is one element shorter than p and the first element of f1 corresponds to the second element of x, we need to concatenate 0.2 to f1 to generate f such that the first element of f is equal to 0.2 and the second element of f (which is also the first element of f1) corresponds to the second element of x.

Logical Operators

Logical operators are applied over logical matrices. These operations again are elementwise and result in a matrix of the same size. The most common logical operators are & (AND), | (OR), NOT (~). The following example will compute the AND of two logical matrices x and y

```
x=[true false true]
y=[false true true]
z=x & y;
```

There are some logical operators which are performed over whole matrices. For example,

```
z=any(x)
```

will be true if any element of x is true.

Relational Operators

Relational operators can be used over numerical matrices to compare them and the result is typically a logical matrix. For example, to compute if each element of x is greater than the corresponding element of y, we can write

```
x=[3 4 5 1 3 5];
y=[3 3 2 5 6 3];
z=x>y;
```

Here z will be the same size as x and its ith element will be 1 if the ith element of x is greater than the ith element of y. Similarly

```
z=x==y
```

will compare each element of x with the corresponding element of y, returning true if they are equal and false otherwise. You can also use z=eq(x,y) to achieve the same result.

Operations for Models

MATLAB also provides operations for various model representations. There are some operations which are valid for many models but may have different meanings and definitions.

For example, consider polynomials. Let $p_1(x) = x + 3$ and $p_2(x) = x + 1$, which can be represented as

```
p1=[1 3]
p2=[1 1]
```

To compute, $p_3(x) = p_1(x)p_2(x)$ we can write

```
p3=conv(p1,p2)
```

which will give

```
p3=[1 4 3]
```

denoting $p_3 = x^2 + 4x + 3$.

We can say that the multiplication operation has a new meaning here and carries a different name, convolution. We can perform polynomial specific operations, such as computing roots

```
f=root(p3)
```

with the result f =[-1 -3] containing the roots of $p_3(x)$ or compute the values of a polynomial at a vector x by

```
x=[1 2 3];
y=polyval(p3,x)
```

resulting in y=[7 15 27].

Let us take another model: the transfer function. Consider two systems defined as

$$S_1 = \frac{1}{s+3}, \; S_2 = \frac{1}{s+1}$$

which can be represented as

```
S1num=1;S1den=[1 3];S1=tf(S1num,S1den);
S2num=1;S2den=[1 1];S1=tf(S2num,S2den);
```

The S3 resulting from the serial connection of these two systems is given as

$$S_3 = S_1 S_2 = \frac{1}{s+3} \times \frac{1}{s+1} = \frac{1}{(s+3)(s+1)}$$

and can be computed in MATLAB as

```
S3=S1*S2;
```

We see that the * operation is overloaded here to give the cascaded output of two systems. Similarly, you can call the step function over a system to evaluate its step response.

```
y=step(S1);
```

All these operations are specific to models. When using these operations, the programmer must keep in mind which model a matrix represents, since MATLAB is not able to differentiate between these matrices and will return the output without throwing an error in most cases. For example, you can call a filter for a transfer function numerator polynomial, but it will not make sense.

There is a wide range of such model representations and model-specific operations. Interested readers should refer to toolbox-specific documentation on the MATLAB website.

Indexing

Indexing of a matrix can be done in several ways. This section will describe different ways of indexing and their pros and cons. For the sake of the following examples, let us assume A is a 4×5 matrix.

Normal Indexing

Normal indexing is the standard indexing of any MATLAB matrix where we need to specify indices in each dimension (for example row and column index for a two dimensional matrix). The following example will extract the element located at the second row and third column of the matrix A:

```
y=A(2,3);
```

Similarly, to change the (3,4)th element of A to 5 we can write

```
A(3,4)=5
```

We can extract multiple columns and rows by specifying the indices as vectors. The following will extract a square matrix containing the second and third rows and third and first columns of the matrix A

```
y=A([2 3],[3 1]);
```

The following will extract all rows and the 5th and 4th columns of the matrix A

```
y=A(:,[5 4])
```

where : denotes all. The following will reverse the column order

```
B=A(:,[end:-1:1])
```

where end is a MATLAB keyword which denotes the length in the dimension it is used.

Linear Indexing

We can also index a matrix by using only one index. The idea is to stack all the elements in one direction, proceeding columnwise as shown in Figure 2-3, indexing the entries by the numbers indicated. For example, we can linearly index A as in Figure 2-3 and we can index (2,3) by 10 using

```
y=A(10).
```

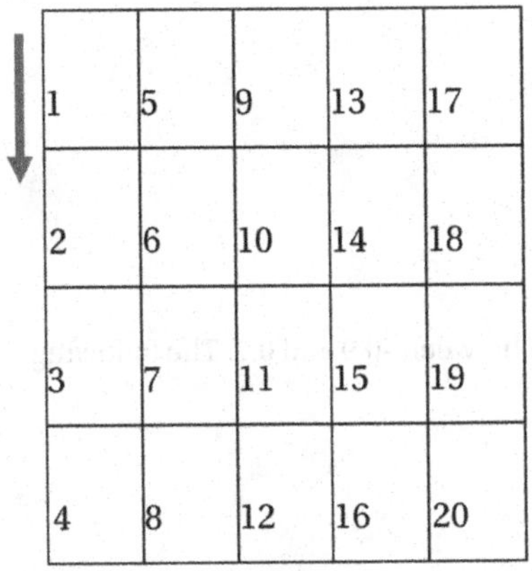

1	5	9	13	17
2	6	10	14	18
3	7	11	15	19
4	8	12	16	20

Figure 2-3. Linear indexing order in a 2D matrix

As for normal indexing, we can also use vectors to index multiple elements. For example, the following code will extract the diagonal of A

```
y=A(1:5:20)
```

Logical Indexing

Logical indexing or indexing by a logical variable is among the best features of MATLAB and this combined with relational operators can make programs very concise and elegant. Suppose I is matrix of the same size as A with true and false entries then

```
B=A(I)
```

will give a matrix containing only those elements of A for which the corresponding elements of I are true. The matrix I can be formed by using a relational operator. For example, suppose we want to extract all those elements from A which are bigger than 5. We first compute I by

```
I=A>5
```

then we index A by I

```
B=A(I)
```

where B will contain only those elements of A which are bigger than 5. Similarly, to replace each element of A which is bigger than 10 with 5, we can write

```
A(A>10)=5
```

Let us see some examples which use the tricks we have learnt so far.

Clipping a Signal

Suppose a signal x(t) is given as

```
t=0:.01:2*pi
x=sin(2*pi*t);
```

Suppose we apply this signal to a clipper circuit which can only pass a signal between -0.9 and 0.7. The following operation will generate the equivalent output y(t)

```
y=x;
y(y>0.7)  = 0.7;
y(y<-0.9) = -0.9;
```

Halving a Matrix

```
A=rand(100,100);
B=A(1:2:end,1:2:end);
```

Vectorization

It should be clear by now that MATLAB is designed for vector and matrix operations. You can often speed up your M-file code by using vectorizing algorithms that take advantage of this design. Vectorization means converting for and while loops to equivalent vector or matrix operations to speed up computations. We will learn more about this in this section.

Recall that we can compute the cube of each element of a matrix via

```
y=x.^3.
```

We can achieve the same via a traditional programming loop

```
for i=1:length(x)
      y(i)=x(i)^3
end
```

It is easy to see that the first method is short and elegant. But as well as being short, the first one is also efficient. Using the first method, MATLAB needs to call the java function only once with the whole vector while in the second method, MATLAB calls the Java function multiple times, once for each element. This difference in fact becomes more prominent when working with large matrices. The use of functions/operators over whole matrices to avoid loops is known as vectorization. In this section we will learn some vectorization tricks via a few examples.

Example 1. Creating C such that C(i,j)=A(i)^B(j)

Suppose A $(1 \times m)$ and B $(n \times 1)$ are vectors and we are interested in generating a matrix C $(n \times m)$ with elements $C(i, j) = A(i)^{B(j)}$.

We will first replicate A n times in rows to make it an $n \times m$ matrix Ar. Then we will replicate B m times in columns so it also becomes an $n \times m$ matrix Br. Now we can perform Ar.^Br to get C. We can see that $C(i, j) = Ar(i, j)^{Br(i,j)} = A(i)'$ as $Ar(i, j) = A(i)$ and $Br(i, j) = B(j)$.

```
Ar=repmat(A,n,1);
Br=repmat(B,1,m);
C=Ar.^Br;
```

Example 2. Calculating the Sum of Harmonics

Suppose we want to compute the signal y(t) given as

$$y(t) = \sum_{N=1}^{10} \frac{1}{2N-1} \sin\left[2\pi (2n-1)50t\right]$$

for the range t=0 to 0.6.

First we try to solve this problem using for loops

```
t = 0:0.001:0.6;
n=1:2:19;
y=0;
for i=n
  y=y+(1/i)*sin(2*pi*i*50*t)
end
```

Now let us try using vectorization. We need to understand that we need two dimensions because there is a time vector (column or horizontal dimension) and the frequency is also varying (row or vertical dimension).

```
n=[1:2:19]';
t=0:.001:0.6;
```

Now we perform a matrix multiplication (not elementwise multiplication) to generate a grid

```
h=n*t;
```

Here h has 10 rows: one row for each frequency and each column represents a time instant. The following

```
g=sin(2*pi*50*h);
```

will compute the signal for each possible frequency and time instant. We want to divide each row by the corresponding frequency from the vector n but we cannot use elementwise division of g by n because n has only one column while g has multiple columns. We observe that each row needs to be divided by the same element n(i) so we replicate n(i) so that the size of n becomes equal to the size of g and all elements of each row of n are the same as the first element of that row. The command

```
n_new=repmat(n,1,size(g,2));
```

will produce the desired matrix. Finally, we can sum each row of the division output columnwise to sum all the frequencies for each time instant.

```
x=sum(g./n_new);
```

Example 3. Conversion to Matrix Operations

Suppose we need to compute a vector A such that $A_i = \sum_m w_k B_{km}$ where w is a vector and B is a matrix. This can equivalently be computed as

```
A=w*B;
```

Example 4. Selective Inversion

Consider the following example. Let A equal[1 2 0 6 4 0 2] and suppose we are interested in constructing the vector B such that

$$B(i) = \begin{cases} \dfrac{1}{A(i)} & \text{if } A(i) \neq 0 \\ 0 & \text{if } A(i) = 0 \end{cases}$$

We will first make B equal to A. Then we will select those elements of B which are not 0 to obtain C. Then we will invert these elements to obtain D. Then we will reassign only these values (i.e. elements in D) to their original indices (the indices corresponding to non-zero elements of B).

```
A=[1 2 0 6 4 0 2];
B=A;
C=B(B~=0);
D=1./C;
B(B~=0)=D;
```

The answer is B=[1 1/2 0 1/6 1/4 0 1/2].
We see that we sometimes need to apply logical indexing multiple times.

Tips for Performance Improvement

Let's review some tips for performance improvement.

Vectorization

As discussed, vectorization is very helpful in reducing computational time. It also makes code elegant and short. Sometimes, when there are multiple loops and some loops cannot be avoided, we should still try to vectorize as many loops as we can. Consider the following example where we want to compute the factorial of each element of the vector x=[2 3 7 4].

First Attempt: Two Loops

```
for i=1:4
            s=1;
                for j=1:x(i)
                    s=s*j;
        end
            A(i)=s;
end
```

Second Attempt: One Loop

```
for i=1:4
A(i)=prod(1:x(i));
end
```

Third Attempt: No Loop

```
mx=max(x);
S=1:mx;
r=[1 cumprod(S)];
A=r(x);
```

Preallocating Arrays

There are cases when loops cannot be avoided. In such cases, we should still make an effort to reduce the computational time by other means. For example, when a variable changes its size at each iteration, it is suggested to pre-allocate it a fixed size to improve the performance and computational time.

Fixed Type Variables

Although MATLAB lets you change the type of a variable within a program, for best performance it is recommended that you should not do it frequently. Changing the class or array shape of an existing variable slows MATLAB down as it must take extra time to process it. When you need to store data of a different type, it is advisable to create a new variable.

CHAPTER 3

Numerical Techniques

In practical real life engineering designs, we often come across problems which consist of numerical operations such as integration or differentiation. For example, in a standard tracing of a robotic arm, the computation of the total error involves integration of instantaneous errors. While mathematical problems require analytic solutions which are sometimes very hard or impossible to obtain, most engineering problems require only numerical solutions. Sometimes the variation of values with parameters is considered sufficient instead of actually finding the closed form relation in terms of parameters. Such a method which involves the numerical computation of the solution is known as a numerical method. These methods form the backbone of engineering and are widely available in MATLAB. In the present chapter, we will study a few basic numerical techniques with which almost all numerical analysis can be done.

One of the prime concerns in numerical methods is that computation platforms only support discrete data. There is no sinusoid signal in numerical software, but only time sampled data of a sinusoidal signal. You can increase the sampling rate to make it closer to a continuous signal, but true continuity can never be achieved. The most important thing in discrete representations is step size and sampling with such a step size gives a sequence of numbers with which we represent the data in MATLAB.

Differentiation

Recall that differentiation of any continuous function f(x) with respect to x is defined as

$$f'(x) = \lim_{h \to 0} \frac{f(x+h) - f(x)}{h}$$

and f'(x) is known as the derivative of f. For discrete level methods, h can be small but can never be too close to 0. Instead, we choose a very small value (sufficiently small) and compute the derivative with that h. The accuracy of computation is dependent on the value of h. However, a small h size will generate large sized vectors when sampling. It is generally found that with sufficiently small h, we can achieve an accuracy which is accurate enough for all practical purposes. However, what the sufficient value of h is must be determined by taking care of the nonlinearity of the function and sample points.

Let us compute the derivative of the function $f(x) = e^{-x} \sin x$. We will first choose a value of h and then compute $\frac{1}{h}[f(x+h) - f(x)]$ as the derivative.

We will first make a function func which defines the objective function:

```
function y=func(x)
y=sin(x).*exp(-x.^2);
```

You can easily guess the implementation for the discrete time differentiation of func:

```
x=4;h=0.01;
ddxofy=1/h*(func(x+h)-func(x));
```

27

We can repeat the above computation to compute the derivative for a whole range, say [0:.01:1]. Let us loop over the x range and calculate the derivative over all points using the above computation,

```
i=1;h=0.01;xrange=0:h:1;
for x=xrange
        ddxofy(i)= 1/h*(func(x+h)-func(x));
        y(i)=func(x);i=i+1;
end
plot(xrange,y);
hold on;
plot(xrange,ddxofy);
```

Figure 3-1 shows the output MATLAB displays. We can see that even if we don't know the analytic form of the derivative, we can see the behavior of the derivative and can easily find its value at any x.

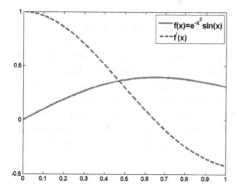

Figure 3-1. Plot of the function $e^{-x^2} \sin x$ with its derivative

The following example attempts to perform the same operation via vectorization. We first construct a vector x with elements distance h apart, then we compute the function over the whole vector and then subtract the adjacent element's function values to get f(x+h)-f(x) and finally divide by h. We can use the diff function, which computes the adjacent differences. For example,

```
x=[1 3 4 2 4];
y=diff(x);
```

will give y=[2 1 -2 2], which has one element less than the original vector. Using diff, we can implement the following

```
x=[0:h:1+h];
y=func(x);
ddxofy=diff(y)/h;
x=x(1:end-1);
```

Since diff reduces the length by 1, we need to reconstruct x such that x and ddxofy have the same size and maintain the element-to-element correspondence. One approach is to remove the last element as performed in the above implementation. Another approach can be to center the interval via the following code

```
x=(x(1:end-1)+x(2:end))/2;
```

Another important aspect in all such computations is the selection of the step size. h should be small enough to give a good approximate solution, but if h is smaller than such "good" h it will cause an unnecessarily high computation time due to the increased size of the vector, without any significant improvement in accuracy.

Partial Differentiation

We can perform the same steps for multivariable functions to compute the partial derivative with respect to each variable. Consider the objective function

$$f(u,v) = \exp(-u^2 - v^2)$$

We will first define an anonymous function to represent the objective function

```
f=@(u,v) exp(-u.^2-v.^2)
```

Notice the use of dots to make the function vectorized so that it can be directly applied to a whole matrix or vector to compute the function value elementwise. Now, since the function has two inputs, its representation will be two-dimensional. Instead of constructing the vector, we will construct a 2D grid with one dimension representing u and the other v, with the help of meshgrid

```
urange=[0:.01:1];
vrange=xrange;
[U V]=meshgrid(urange,vrange);
```

U and V are two-dimensional matrices such that $(U(i,j), V(i,j))$ denotes the x, y coordinate of the (i,j)th point in the Cartesian plane. We can evaluate the whole function over the grid

```
fvalue=f(U,V);
```

Now we can call diff in the row direction (second dimension) (i.e. the difference of adjacent elements in the same row) to compute $f(u+du,v) - f(u,v)$ and divide by du to get $\dfrac{\partial f}{\partial u}$

```
dduofz=diff(z,1,2);
```

Similarly, for $\dfrac{\partial f}{\partial v}$ we need to evaluate diff in the first dimension:

```
ddvofdz=diff(z,1,1);
```

or just

```
ddvofdz=diff(z);
```

MATLAB also provides a function called gradient to evaluate the same

```
[px,py] = gradient(z,ustepsize,vstepsize);
```

Similarly, we can compute the derivative of higher dimensional matrices and higher order derivatives. Let us consider, for example, the computation of a Jacobian. We just need to do the previous operation for each function output component. Recall that the Jacobian is defined as

$$J = \begin{bmatrix} \dfrac{\partial f_1}{\partial u} & \dfrac{\partial f_2}{\partial u} \\ \dfrac{\partial f_1}{\partial v} & \dfrac{\partial f_2}{\partial v} \end{bmatrix}$$

Let's consider the function

$$f(u,v) = (u^2 + v^2, uv)$$

We can compute the Jacobian via the following code

```
range = -2:0.2:2;
[x,y] = meshgrid(range);
Z1 = (x.^2 + y.^2);
[px1,py1] = gradient(z1,.2,.2);
Z2 = (x.^2 - y.^2);
[px2,py2] = gradient(z2,.2,.2);
J(:,:,1)=[px1];
J(:,:,2)=[px2];
J(:,:,3)=[py1];
J(:,:,4)=[py2];
```

Computing Higher Derivatives

Applying the same steps multiple times will result in higher order derivatives. However, we should remember that diff decreases the vector size by 1, so we should rectify the length at each differentiation step by either of the two methods discussed earlier. The following example describes this process

```
x=[0:h:1+h];
y=func(x);
ddxofy=diff(y)/h;
x1=1/ 2 (x(1:end-1)+x(2:end));
d2dx2y=diff(ddxofy)/h;
x2=1/ 2 (x1(1:end-1)+x1(2:end));
```

Integration

In a discrete simulation environment, definite integration is just a fine summation. For example, consider the following function,

$$f(x) = sin\ 2x$$

and the integral $I = \int_0^1 \sin 2x\, dx$, which gives the area under the curve in Figure 3-2(a), and which can be approximated by the shaded area in Figure 2(b). Tuning the value of h, this approximation can be made more accurate. In mathematical terms, the same approximation can be represented as

$$I \approx \sum_{n=0}^{1/h} h \sin 2nh$$

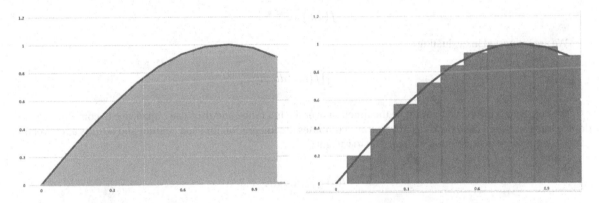

Figure 3-2. *Integral of sin(x)*

In MATLAB or any numerical software, we cannot implement the continuous representation but we can always implement the discrete representation and evaluate the approximation with some error. Let us first define the x vector and evaluate the function over it

```
h=1/100;
x=[0:h:1];
z=sin(2x);
```

and then compute the summation via

```
intz=sum(z)*h;
```

which equals 0.4639, which is very close to the actual value of 0.4597. Since trapezoidal division-based approximation is more accurate, MATLAB provides the `trapz` function, which computes the summation by trapezoidal area approximation instead of rectangle area approximation.

```
intz=trapz(x,z);
```

This results in 0.4596, which is far closer to the actual value. Indefinite integrals can also be computed in numerical form. For other values, you cannot compute the exact analytical form of an indefinite integral, but you can find its numerical values at different x and plot its variation, which may be sufficient from an engineering perspective.

```
h=1/100;
x=[0:h:1];
z=sin(2x);
intz=cumsum(z)*h;
x1=x(1:end-1);
```

Multi-dimensional Integration

Let us consider a two-dimensional function and integration over both the variables. This can be extended to higher dimensional functions. Consider the function

$$f(u,v) = e^{-u^2-v}$$

We are interested in evaluating

$$I = \int_0^1 \int_0^1 f(u,v)\,du\,dv$$

We construct a meshgrid to evaluate the function over the full range and then use trapz twice to compute the double integral. When used on 2D matrices, trapz computes the integration for each column and returns a row vector which is equivalent to integration with respect to v to get

$$I(u) = \int_0^1 f(u,v)dv.$$

We can apply trapz again on I(u) to compute the integral:

```
[U V]=meshgrid(range);
f=func(U,V);
Iu=trapz(V,f);
I=trapz(U(1,:),Iu);
```

We see that, since each of the rows of U are the same and Iu is just a vector, we need only the first row of U to serve as x in trapz.

Integration Over an Infinite Range

If the function is such that its integral over the infinite range can be approximated by an integral over a finite range, we can compute the integration using MATLAB. One example of such a function is any function which decreases quickly as $X \to \infty$. The crucial point here is to find the finite range which can approximate the integral with small errors.

Consider the following function

$$y = e^{-2x}$$

Suppose we are interested in computing the integral over the range 0 to infinity. Since the function decreases fast enough, let us compute the integral over the ranges [0 2], [0 10] and [0 100].

```
upperlimit=[2 10 100];
for i=1:3
        x=0:.01:upperlimit(i);
        y=exp(-2*x);
        I(i)=trapz(x,y);
end
```

You can see that I(2) and I(3) are almost the same and are different from I(1). So [0 10] is a good enough range for this particular example of integration. Moreover, as usual, you don't want to take a bigger range (for example, [0 100] here) if the same results can be obtained with a lower range (for example, [0 10] here) because a bigger range will result in a bigger vector x which will slow down the computation without any significant improvement in accuracy.

Multidimensional Integration over Non-rectangular Intervals

The integration need not be over a rectangular area. Consider the following integral

$$y = \int_R e^{-x^y - y^2} \, dx \, dy$$

$$R = \{(x,y): 10 > x > 0, x > y > 0\}$$

which is equivalent to the integral

$$y = \int_{R'} g(x,y) \, dx \, dy$$

$$R' = \{(x,y): 10 > x > 0, 10 > y > 0\}$$

$$g(x,y) = \begin{cases} e^{-x^y - y^2} & \text{for } x > y \\ 0 & \text{otherwise} \end{cases}$$

The procedure is almost the same, but we don't have non-rectangular matrices in MATLAB. So we define an auxiliary function $g(x,y)$. We first find a rectangular area which covers the given region R and construct a meshgrid over this rectangular area.

```
range=0:.01:10;
[U V]=meshgrid(range);
```

Then we compute the value of the function f for all grid points in the same fashion.

```
f=func(U,V);
```

To get the value of the function g from the function f, we just make all the values corresponding to grid points outside the given interval equal to zero.

```
g=f;
g(U<V)=0;
```

Now we can compute the integral of this modified function g over the rectangular region which will be equal to the integral of the original function f over the original non-rectangular region.

```
Iu=trapz(V,g);
I=trapz(U(1,:),Iu);
```

Solving Equations

In this section, we will talk about solving a single variable equation which may contain linear or nonlinear functions. For example, suppose we want to solve

$$f(x) = 0$$

In other words, we are interested in finding the zeros of a function. This problem is one of the classical problems of numerical analysis. It has variety of applications, such as finding the minimum of a function by finding the zeros of its first derivative, finding the equilibrium of a system, etc.

Polynomial Functions

If the function is a polynomial, its zeros can be found using the roots function. Refer to the second chapter or a MATLAB reference on polynomials for how polynomials can be defined. For example, if we want to find the roots of $p(x) = x^4 + 2x^3 + 2x^2 + x$, we do the following:

```
P=[1 2 2 0 1];
x=roots(P);
```

Zeros of a General Function

MATLAB provides a very wide set of functions to solve numerical problems, especially for finding zeros and optimization. We will explore more of them throughout the book. Here, we will focus on a special function called fzero, which is used to find the solution of a one variable function.

Consider the simple function

$$f(x) = x - cos(x)$$

The important thing to remember is that MATLAB will attempt to solve this equation by numerical techniques. Numerical techniques are very different to analytic techniques. To illustrate the difference, let us consider the following simple example

$$x - 5 = 2$$

An analytic approach is to transfer -5 to the RHS to get $x = 7$.

However, a numerical approach is iterative. The simple procedure will start with an initial guess $x = 1$ and compute its value $f(x) = -4$ which is less than 2. It will first increase the value of x to 5 and compute $f(x) = -2$. It will observe that f(x) is getting closer to the RHS, so it will increase further to 9 and observe that the function value $f(x) = 4$ has exceeded the RHS. It would then decrease the value to the mid-value of $x = 7$ and find that $f(x) = 2$ matches the RHS and output the answer. This was a linear approach and therefore the solution algorithm was very easy. Even in such a case, the number of steps to reach the answer depends on the initial guess. As the equation degree or complexity increases, the need for a more sophisticated algorithm becomes evident. Also, for some cases, the choice of initial guess may affect the output you get.

Now let us concentrate on solving the original problem with fzero. Like any numerical method, to call fzero, we need an initial guess x0,

```
X0=1;
x=fzero('cos(x)-x',x0);
```

The underlying algorithm behind fzero is very simple and consists of two steps.

Interval search step: It first searches for a value x1 for which the function value differs in sign from the function value at x0. When it finds such a value, it sets the search interval as [x0 x1].

Zero search step: It now uses interpolation to find an approximate zero x2. If f(x2) has the same sign as f(x1), the next search interval is set to [x0 x2] otherwise the new search interval is [x2 x1]. It then repeats the process. It may need many iterations to reach the desired level of accuracy.

If we know an interval for which the function values differs in sign at its boundaries, we can directly specify this interval rather than an initial guess at the solution

```
x=fzero('cos(x)-x',[0 1]);
```

A numerical method may have multiple options. For example, termination condition specifications, such as when to terminate or what the tolerance error is after which the iteration should terminate, or display specifications. You can specify these specifications using optimset. For example, you can specify the tolerance by writing

```
x=fzero('cos(x)-x',x0,optimset('TolX',1e-3));
```

The optimset function returns an option structure which contains control parameters for the fzero function. More information can be seen by typing help optimset and fzero. Similarly, we can instruct fzero to display each iteration result in the command window by setting display in optimset

```
x=fzero('cos(x)-x',x0,optimset('TolX',1e-3,'Display','iter'));
```

The result would be something like

```
Search for an interval around 0 containing a sign change:
Func-count a f(a)b f(b) Procedure
       1  010  1 initial interval
       3 -0.0282843 1.0278  0.0282  0.971316 search
       5 -0.04 1.0392  0.04 0.9592 search
       7 -0.0565685    1.0549  0.0565  0.941832 search
       9 -0.08 1.07680.08    0.916802 search
  11 -0.113137    1.1067  0.1131  0.88047       search
  13 -0.16 1.14723 0.16     0.827227 search
  15 -0.226274 1.20078 0.2262   0.748235 search
  17 -0.32 1.26924 0.32 0.629235 search
  19 -0.4525481.3518  0.45254 0.446787 search
  21 -0.64 1.4421  0.64  0.162096 search
  23 -0.9050971.5227  0.9050  -0.287487 search
Search for a zero in the interval [-0.905097, 0.905097]:
Func-count x f(x)Procedure
  23  0.905097      -0.287487 initial
  24  0.617610.197656    interpolation
  25  0.734737        0.00727045 interpolation
  26  0.739099      -2.37581e-005   interpolation
  27  0.739099      -2.37581e-005   interpolation
```

fzero also accepts function handles

```
f=@(x) sin(x)-.4;
x=fzero(f,0);
```

or

```
x=fzero(@myfunc1,[0 1]);
```

where myfunc1 is defined in myfunc1.m

If the function is dependent not only on x but also on a few more inputs, say c, and you want to know the value of x such that $f(x,c)=0$, you can define an anonymous function g(x) = $f(x, c)$ for fixed x and fzero must be called over this g(x). The following example describes the same method for the variable c.

```
for c=0:1:10
g=@(x) sin(x)-c/10;
x(c+1)=fzero(g,[0 3.14]);
end
```

Interpolation

When we have discrete data instead of continuous data, the need to reconstruct the continuous data is evident. For example, with the knowledge of output voltage sampled at .1 seconds starting from t=0, can we compute (approximate) the value at 2.314 sec? In many cases we don't have data for all the points, but only at some. In that case, the common problem is to generate the data for other points. This procedure is known as interpolation. In other words, given x_n for $n = 1,2,\ldots k+n$ and y_n values for n=1,2,...k, we need y_n for $n = k+1, k+2,\ldots k+n$ where $y_n = f(x_n)$.

One-dimensional Interpolation

One-dimensional interpolation can be done using the interp1 function. Suppose we know the vector Y containing the function values y=f(x) at x values contained in X and we wish to evaluate the function over a finer grid XI. We can do so by using the interp1 function in the following format:

```
YI = interp1(X, Y, XI, method),
```

where the vectors X and Y are the vectors holding the x- and the y- coordinates of points to be interpolated, respectively, XI is a vector holding the points of evaluation, i.e., new points, and method is an optional string specifying an interpolation method.

The following methods work with the function interp1.

Nearest Neighbor Interpolation

Method = 'nearest'. Produces a locally piecewise constant interpolant.

Linear Interpolation

Method = 'linear'. Produces a piecewise linear interpolant.

Cubic Spline Interpolation

Method = 'spline'. Produces a cubic spline interpolant.

Cubic Interpolation

Method = 'cubic'. Produces a piecewise cubic polynomial.
   In this example, the y data for the $0:\dfrac{\pi}{5}:\pi$ x points are given as $(x_k, y_k) = \left(\dfrac{k\pi}{5}, \sin\left(\dfrac{2\pi k}{5} \right) \right)$

```
x = 0:pi/5:pi;
y = sin(2.*x);
```

which need to be interpolated using the method of interpolation 'nearest' . The interpolant is evaluated at the following points

```
xi = 0:pi/100:pi;
yi = interp1(x, y, xi, 'nearest');
```

Spline Interpolation

The MATLAB function spline is designed for computations with cubic splines ($n = 3$) that are twice continuously differentiable ($k = 2$) on the interval. The MATLAB command

```
yi = spline(x, y, xi)
```

evaluates a cubic spline s(x) at points stored in the array xi.

Data Fitting and Polynomial Interpolation

One method of interpolation is to fit an nth degree polynomial to the data and then calculate polynomial values at interpolated points. This can be done easily as

```
p=polyfit(x,y,n);
yi=polyval(p,xi);
```

   For example, suppose we are given data x and y as

```
x=0:.01:1;
y=x.^3+2*x+0.02*rand(size(x));
```

Let us not worry about how x and y are generated and assume the vectors are given to us. We can fit a third degree polynomial to this data as

```
p=polyfit(x,y,3)
```

which gives us p = [0.9686 0.0489 1.9758 0.014]. Once we get the polynomial coefficients, the values at any x or range can be computed as

```
xi=0:.005:2;
yi=polyval(p,xi)
```

Figure 3-3 shows the MATLAB output when x,y and xi,yi are plotted on the same graph. Since the limits of xi are beyond x, it is in fact an extrapolation.

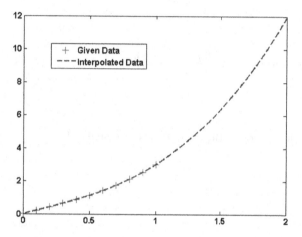

Figure 3-3. *Polynomial interpolation (extrapolation)*

Arbitrary Interpolation

You may need to interpolate your data according to your model. This problem comes under model parameter analysis and can be solved using optimization. We will revisit this method in later chapters.

CHAPTER 4

Visualization

Visualization is an important part of any engineering application and can be used to provide insights into design problems or to examine the performance of any solution method. In this chapter, we will talk about basic plotting techniques in MATLAB and how to visualize complex results using them, including animation. MATLAB provides a wide range of functions for 2D and 3D plots of various kinds and also enables you to annotate or decorate the plots with auxiliary functions.

Line Plots

2D line plots can be used to represent the relation between variables x and y which can be in the form of a function $y = f(x)$ or a dataset (x, y). To plot any relation, MATLAB only needs the values x and y. Let us start with a simple example where values of (x, y) are obtained from some experiment and given directly to MATLAB. For example, a student in a physics class performs Ohm's experiment to compute the resistance of a given device. He records the following observations where I is the current in the device when a voltage V is applied across it.

V (V)	0	0.5	1.0	1.5	2.3
I (mA)	0	2	4.1	5.8	9

This data can be represented in MATLAB by the following matrices

```
V=[0 0.5 1.0 1.5 2.3];
I=[0 2 4.1 5.8 9];
```

Remember that the matrices V and I are data matrixes and have an elementwise one-to-one correspondence with each other, so that the third element in V corresponds to the third element in I. To visualize this relation, we can use the plot function with the x and y matrices as input in the following way

```
plot(V,I)
```

which gives the plot between V and I. (See Figure 4-1.)

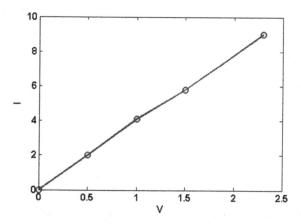

Figure 4-1. *Plot I versus V*

The functioning of the plot function is very straightforward, it just makes the pairs (x_i, y_i) by taking corresponding elements from the x and y matrices and plots them on a Cartesian plane, joining them by straight lines. Of course, x and y must be of the same size. In the similar way, we can also plot the function $y = f(x)$. Since computer tools can only work with discrete data, we need to represent this function as discrete data. For that, we make an x vector with values separated by a small gap and then compute the function values at those x to get the y vector.

```
x=0:.01:2*pi;
y=x.*exp(-x);
plot(x,y);
```

If the x values are very closely packed, the plot will look like a continuous plot (see Figure 4-2a). Remember the dot operation is the elementwise operation on the data matrices. How close the gap should be depends on the non-linearity of the function. For example, a linear function $y = 2x + 3$ can be plotted with just two x values, while a function like $y = xe^{-x}$ would require many points for a smooth and accurate display. Figure 4-2b shows the function with gap $\dfrac{\pi}{10}$ and it is not smooth, even with 21 points.

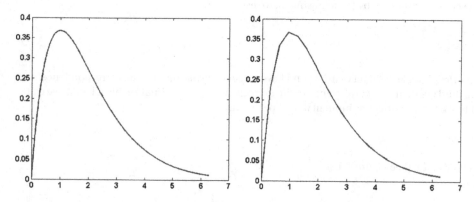

Figure 4-2. *Plotting a continuous function*

Plot Options

We can specify different properties like color, line style, marker type, etc. while plotting. If we pass a string with three characters representing one character from each of the following columns to specify color, marker type and line style, the plot will be drawn with those properties.

r	Red	.	Point marker	-	Solid line
b	Blue	s	Rectangle marker	--	Dashed line
c	Cyan	o	Circle	:	Dotted line
k	Black	x	Xmark	-.	dashdot
g	Green	+	Plus	(none)	No line
y	Yellow	*	Star		
w	White	d	Diamond		
m	Magenta				

We can plot x versus cos(x) with red color solid plots, and with pentagon markers, using the following code

```
plot([0:.1:1],cos([0:.1:1]), 'rp-');
```

We can skip some characters from the specification string. Suppose we want to draw the plot in red. We can do this using a string with just one more parameter

```
plot(X,Y,'r');
```

You can also use property and value pair specification in the following way

```
plot(X,Y, PropertyName, PropertyValue)
```

to specify more properties for a plot. For example, to increase the linewidth of a lineplot, we can write

```
plot(X,Y,'LineWidth', 10);
```

Similarly

```
plot(X,Y,'LineWidth', 10,'MarkerSize', 4);
```

You can specify properties and their values for plots. The following properties and sample values are important to keep in mind for quick reference:

```
Color: [0 0 1]
EraseMode: 'normal'
LineStyle: '-'
LineWidth: 0.5000
Marker: 'none'
MarkerSize: 6
```

Multiple Plots

We can plot multiple curves on the same figure by using the hold on command. By default, if we plot a curve, MATLAB deletes the previous plot, if there is one. The command hold on forces MATLAB to keep the previous plot and adds the new plot to the figure. For example, the following code will generate two overlapping cos and sin curves colored red and blue, respectively.

```
t=0:.01:2*pi;
y1=sin(t);
y2=cos(t);
plot(t,y1,'b');
hold on
plot(t,y2,'r')
```

Annotations

We can add text, labels, and legends to add more information to a plot. To add an axis label, we can use xlabel or ylabel, respectively, for the x and y axes

```
xlabel('time')
ylabel('response');
```

whereas the following commands will add a title and legend to the plot

```
title('time response of the system S')
legend({'system S'});
```

To add text, we can use the command text by specifying the string and the location in the figure where we want the text to appear:

```
xlocation=0.1;
ylocation=0.2;
text(xlocation,ylocation,'threshold')
```

Handles

We can also edit the properties of a figure or axis after they are drawn. MATLAB assigns a number to each graphical object which is known as its handle and which can be used to point to that object later. For example, to plot $y = x^2$ first and then change the line color to black we can do this by using the following lines of code

```
x=[0:.01:1];y=x.^2;
h=plot(x,y);
set(h,'Color',[0 0 0]);
```

where h is handle of the plot object. The function set sets the color property of the object pointed to by h to [0 0 0], which is the value for black in RGB.

2D plots

Other than line plots, there are other different types of plots in 2D which are mentioned in the following table.

Line Graphs	Bar Graphs	Area Graphs	Direction Graphs	Radial Graphs	Scatter Graphs
plot	bar	area	feather	Polar	scatter
plotyy	barh	pie	quiver	Rose	spy
loglog	hist	fill	comet	compass	plotmatrix
semilogx	errorbar	contourf		ezpolar	
stairs	stem	image			
ezplot		pcolor			
ezcontour		ezcontourf			

The syntax and usage of almost all the functions mentioned above are very similar to the plot function. We will describe a couple of them. For example, to make a scatter plot of x,y, we would write

```
x=rand(10,1);
y=rand(10,1)+.1*rand(10,1);
scatter(x,y);
```

Similarly, to create a bar graph of the following height data in a class of 50,

Height	5'-5'4"	5'4"-5'8"	5'8"-6'	6'-6'4"	6'4"-6-8"
No of Students	5	15	15	11	4

we can execute the following code:

```
nofS=[5 15 15 11 4];
h=bar(1:5,nofS);
```

Quiver Plots

Quiver plots are used to show the flow at different grid points. It requires four matrices X, Y, U and V and at each grid point (X_{ij}, Y_{ij}), it puts an arrow pointing in the (U_{ij}, V_{ij}) direction (see Figure 4-3).

```
range = -2:0.2:2;
[x,y] = meshgrid(range);
z1 = (x.^2 + y.^2);
[px1,py1] = gradient(z1,.2,.2);
quiver(x,y,px1,py1);
```

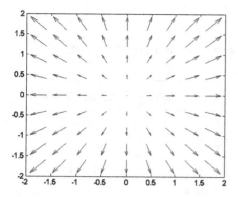

Figure 4-3. *Quiver plots*

3D Plots

3D plots are primarily used to represent a function of two variables in the form of a surface. MATLAB defines a surface via the z-coordinates of points above a rectangular grid in the x-y plane. The plot is formed by joining adjacent points with straight lines.

As we generate the x vector first for the linear plot of the function $y = f(x)$, the first step in displaying a function of two variables, $z = f(x,y)$, is to generate base grid matrices X and Y such that each corresponding pair (X_{ij}, Y_{ij}) represents a point on the 2D grid. The X and Y matrices consist of repeated rows and columns, respectively, over the domain of the function. Then these pairs are used to evaluate and graph the function.

First we specify the range of the x axis and y axis via the x and y vectors. The meshgrid function transforms the domain specified by the two vectors, x and y, into matrices X and Y. As discussed, we then use these matrices to evaluate functions of two variables by elementwise operations. The rows of X are copies of the vector x and the columns of Y are copies of the vector y.

To illustrate the use of meshgrid, consider the distance function R. To evaluate this function between -8 and 8 in both x and y, you need pass only one vector argument to meshgrid, which is then used in both directions.

```
[X,Y] = meshgrid(-8:.5:8);
R = sqrt(X.^2 + Y.^2);
```

To plot R over X and Y, we can write (see Figure 4-4a)

```
surf(X,Y,R);
```

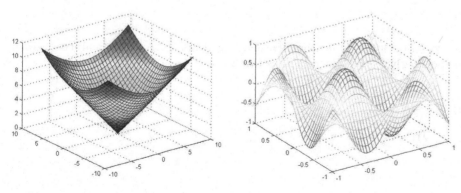

Figure 4-4. *3D plots: surf and mesh*

44

Ensure that X, Y and R are matrices of same size. Instead of the function surf we can also use the mesh command which only generates a mesh without coloring the surface. Try the following command to generate a wave on the sea (see Figure 4-4b).

```
[X,Y] = meshgrid(-1:.05:1,-1:.05:1);
R = sin(4*X).*sin(4* Y);
mesh(X,Y,R)
```

You can also use a parametric representation to calculate x, y and z as in the following example, which plots a sphere

```
k = 5; n = 2^k-1;
theta = pi*(-n:2:n)/n;
phi = (pi/2)*(-n:2:n)'/n;
X = cos(phi)*cos(theta);
Y = cos(phi)*sin(theta);
Z = sin(phi)*ones(size(theta));
colormap([0 0 0;1 1 1])
surf(X,Y,Z)
axis square
```

The main idea is to create matrices X, Y and Z such that the pair consisting of the (i,j) elements of X and Y represents a point in the 2D plane and the (i,j)th element of Z represents the value at this point.

Animations

An animation is just a combination of multiple plots shown one after the other, separated by a time interval sufficiently small to create the illusion that they are continuously changing. We begin with an animation of a small clock with second hand only. The important function we need to know is drawnow.

The command drawnow forces MATLAB to flush the graphics at that instant. By default, if MATLAB sees any plot command in the middle of the execution of a heavy computation, it waits until the computations are done and then shows the graphics. Since we need to see the plots at that instant in order for the animation to vary with time, we can use the drawnow command, which forces MATLAB to show the graphic at that instant only.

A Clock Animation

We create 100 time frames using a for loop. In each frame, we plot the clock outer ring and the hand, but the position of the hand will change at each frame. Since 100 frames shows a full cycle of the hand (1 minute), 1 frame represents a time duration of 1/100 minutes or a $\dfrac{2\pi}{100}$ angular rotation on the clock. At the ith frame, the needle will be just a line between $[0, 0]$ to $\left[-l\cos\dfrac{2\pi i}{100}, -l\sin\dfrac{2\pi i}{100} \right]$ where l is the length of the hand. To create the animation, we would carry out the following steps:

1. Clear the frame

2. Increase the frame number

3. Plot the outer ring of the clock as a circle

4.   Plot the line for the hand

5.   Go to step 1 if the current frame number is less than 100

```
t=0:.01:2*pi;
radius_clock=1;
length_needle=.8;
for i=1:100
        %plot objects of the ith frame
        hold off;
        plot(radius_clock*cos(t),radius_clock*sin(t),...
                                'LineWidth',4);
        hold on;
        plot([0 length_needle*cos(-2*pi*i/100)], ...
                [0 length_needle*sin(-2*pi*i/100)],'LineWidth',2);
    drawnow;
    end
```

The hold off command tells MATLAB to let the previous frame graphics be deleted when the new frame is plotted. The above code generates an animation with the clock needle making one circuit around the clock. See Figure 4-5 for one frame of the whole animation. We can add other clock hands for hours and minutes and use three nested for loops to create the complete clock.

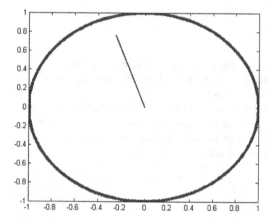

Figure 4-5. *Clock Animation*

Wave Motion

Consider the wave motion of a string $(0 \le x \le 1)$ where the height of a particle located at x is given by

$$w(t,x) = sin(t\omega - kx)$$

Suppose we want to visualize the height of particles situated on the string with varying time ($0 \leq t \leq 1$). As done in the previous example, we first plot a single frame at time i and then repeat it for all frames. At time i, the string looks like a sin wave

$$w_i = sin(-kx + \phi_i)$$

where $\phi_i = i\omega$.

```
X=0:.01:1;
k=3;
omega=100;i=0;
W_i=sin(-k*X+i*omega);
plot(X,W_i,LineWidth',2);
```

Now we iterate the code to plot for i = 0:0.1:10. Here we are plotting only one object, so we don't need to use hold on and therefore no clearing of the figure is required.

```
X=0:.01:1;
k=3;
omega=100;
for i=0:.001:1
        W_i=sin(-k*X+i*omega);
        plot(X,W_i,'LineWidth',2);
        axis([0 1.2 -1.2 1.2])
        drawnow;
end
```

Here the axis command fixes the axis so that at each plot the axis and hence the display frame doesn't move up and down. We will see more examples of animations in later chapters when we learn about simulation and other related techniques.

Movies

We can also create a movie from an animation and save it to an AVI file. Consider the previous example of the wave motion of a string. To create a movie frame from the ith frame, we can use the get frame function in the following way

```
J=1;
for i=0:.01:1
        W_i=sin(-k*X+i*omega);
        plot(X,W_i,'LineWidth',2);
        axis([0 1.2 -1.2 1.2])
        drawnow;
        M(J)=getframe(gcf);
        J=J+1;
end
```

Here gcf is the handle of the current figure and M is the matrix containing all frames. To create the AVI movie containing these frames, we execute the following command

```
movie2avi(M,'moviename.avi');
```

CHAPTER 5

■ ■ ■

Introduction to Simulation

In many cases, to understand the dynamics of a real world system or a function of a physical system, we need to model it and imitate the step by step operation of the system using a computational tool. This step by step imitation of a real world process is known as simulation. The systems can include any physical phenomena such as Brownian motion or the path of a projectile; or man-made devices such as robots or motors. Computational tools developed for simulating a system can be based on hardware or software. In this chapter, we will learn how to simulate in a software-based computation tool, in particular in MATLAB.

One Step Simulations

Although real world processes are infinite time processes, sometimes they can be regarded as one time computations. For example, suppose a projectile is thrown into the sky with velocity $v_x \vec{i} + v_Y \vec{j}$ from the ground.

If we want to know the motion of this projectile or the range covered by it, even though the process evolves with time, we can compute it in one step using motion equations:

Location path:

$$x(t) = v_x t \vec{i} + \left(v_Y t - \frac{1}{2} g t^2 \right) \vec{j}$$

and this can be plotted easily using the following code (see Figure 5-1):

```
v=[10 20];
g=9.8;
%flight time
flighttime=2(v(2))/g;
%range
r=v(1)*flighttime;
%plot projectile path
t=[0:flighttime/100:flighttime];
plot(v(1)*t,v(2)*t-0.5*g*t.^2);
```

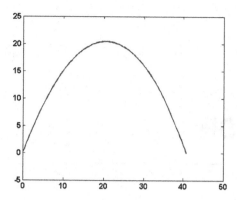

Figure 5-1. *Simulated path of a projectile*

However, when the motion is complex, e.g. affected by many forces or collisions, it is very hard to compute the equations of the path. In such cases we need to simulate the process at small time steps to see how each object moves in each instant. We will see how we can simulate projectile motion using iterative simulations in later sections of this chapter.

In this section, we will consider a simple example from optics which will illustrate the basic technique of one step simulation. Let us assume a point located at $x = a$, $y = 0$. A plane mirror is positioned in the YZ plane at y=0. To compute the reflection, we will take two rays originating from the point and find its reflected ray and finally compute the intersection to find the image (Figure 5-2 shows the results).

```
%Location of the point
a=10;x1=[a 0];
%take first line at theta =120, line in the format y=m1x+c1
t1=120;m1=tand(t1);
c1=0-m1*a;
%hitting point at mirror
A=[0 0*m1+c1];
%reflected light y=mr1x+cr1
mr1=tand(180-t1);cr1=A(2)-  mr1*A(1);
%second ray at t=150
t2=150;m2=tand(t2);
c2=0-m2*a;B=[0 0*m2+c2];
mr2=tand(180-t2);cr2=B(2)-  mr2*B(1);
%intersection of y=mr1x+cr1 and y=mr2x+cr2
xr=(cr2-cr1)/(mr1-mr2);
yr=xr*mr1+cr1;
disp([xr yr]);
```

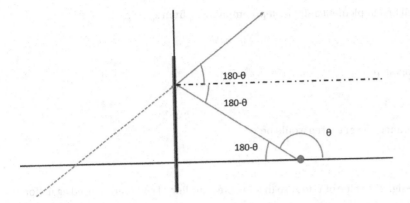

Figure 5-2. *Ray tracing diagram for a point object in front of a plane mirror*

Iterative Methods

First, as a warm up exercise, we discuss some numerical methods which require iterations to be performed. Let us take a simple example of computing the zeros of the following equation:

$$x \sin x - 0.2 = 0$$

There are many techniques available to solve equations of the form $f(x)=0$. One of them is the Newton-Raphson method, which is performed as follows:

1. We begin with a first guess x_0.

2. A better solution of the equation x_1, can be computed as

$$x_1 = x_0 - \frac{f(x_0)}{f'(x_0)}$$

3. Compute $f(x_1)$ and, if it is close enough to 0, terminate the algorithm and output x_1.

4. Now put $x_0 = x_1$ and compute x_1 again by returning to step 2.

The algorithm is terminated when $f(x_1)$ is close enough to zero, let us say when $|f(x_1)|<\epsilon_f$ where ϵ_f is known as the function tolerance and can be arbitrarily defined according to the precision required. In this example, we set it to be equal to 0.001. There can be other termination conditions too, for example, we can terminate the algorithm when the value of x varies by a small difference in two consecutive iterations, in other words if $|x_1 - x_0|<\epsilon_x$. Here ϵ_x is known as the x tolerance. The tolerance can also be defined in relative rather than absolute terms. For example, we can terminate the algorithm when

$$\frac{|x_1 - x_0|}{x_0} < \epsilon_{x,r}.$$

Let us first define the function and its derivative along with some parameters.

```
f=@(x) x.*sin(x)-0.2;
fprime=@(x) sin(x)+x.*cos(x);
x_0=0.1;
tolerance=0.001;
```

To implement the algorithm, we will first implement a single step, computing x_1 from x_0

```
x_1=x_0-f(x_0)/fprime(x_0);
```

Let us compute the error value of this step

```
err_step=abs(f(x_1));
```

Note that if we were using the x tolerance, the err_step would be

```
err_step=abs(x_1-x_0);
```

Now for the next step, we need to assign the value of x_0 to x_1 so that the previous line of code can be used again for the next step when computing the next x_1.

```
x_0=x_1;
```

The whole step will look like

```
x_1=x_0-f(x_0)/fprime(x_0);
err_step=abs(f(x_1));
x_0=x_1;
```

Now this step can be repeated until the tolerance condition is met. The final value of x1 will be the solution. The whole code would look like the following

```
f=@(x) x.*sin(x)-0.2;
fprime=@(x) sin(x)+x.*cos(x);
x_0=0.1;
tolerance=0.001;
err_step=100;
while(err_step>tolerance)
        x_1=x_0-f(x_0)/fprime(x_0);
        err_step=abs(f(x_1));
        x_0=x_1;
end
final_sol=x_1;
```

When we run the above code, we get the answer as 0.4551.

Simulation of Real World Processes

In the previous section, we have seen how to implement an iterative method. Most real world processes are finite or infinite iterations of some steps. Let us first concentrate on discrete processes.

Discrete Processes

A discrete process x[n] is generally represented in the following two forms:

1. Explicit expression of the value of the process at time n as x[n].

    For example: $x[n] = \sin 2pn$.

2. Definition of x[n] in terms of values at previous time steps, known as a time update equation.

    For example: $x[n] = \frac{1}{2}x[n-1] + w[n]$.

We will concentrate on the second definition as the first one is trivial. The following are the important steps used to simulate any real world process.

1. Understand the process and make a mathematical model to compute the time step update equation.

2. Model/generate or acquire the input signal.

3. Implement one time step.

4. Repeat the iterations for the desired time duration.

The following subsections discuss some examples of discrete random processes.

Random Walks

A random walk is a walk or series of steps where each step taken by the object is independent of all previous steps. It is also known as a drunken walk, where the person does not know where to go and each step taken by him is random. We will consider the discrete case in 2D space where four possible steps are allowed:

1. [1 0] : unit step in the direction of the positive X axis

2. [-1 0] : unit step in the direction of the negative X axis

3. [0 1] : unit step in the direction of the positive Y axis

4. [0 -1] : unit step in the direction of the negative Y axis

At each time step, the object chooses a number randomly out of {1,2,3,4} and depending on that number, it will take a step in the corresponding direction. A similar process is followed at each time step and this continues indefinitely. The random walk is the basis of many natural processes, such as Brownian motion.

The update equation is given as

$$r[n] = r[n-1] + [10]1_{w[n]==4} + [-10]1_{w[n]==1} + [01]1_{w[n]==2} + [0-1]1_{w[n]==0};$$

Here $r[n]$ is the location of the point at time step n

$$r[n] = [x[n], y[n]]$$

and $w[n]$ is a random number with value between 1 to 4.

Since it is an iterative process, we will need to use a loop for its simulation. We will first simulate a single step, then we will put a loop around it. A single time step at time n consists of the following four sub-steps.

1. Assign the current position .

2. Generate a random number $w[n]$ to select the direction of motion, which requires two bits $[w_1, w_2]$ of a random Bernoulli variable. These two values combined will select the direction as follows:

```
b=rand(1,2);
w=b>0.5;
if w==1
            rstep=[1 0];
elseif w(1)==1
        rstep=[0 1];
elseif w(2)==1
        rstep=[-1 0];
else
        rstep=[0 -1];
end
```

Remember if you put w==1 as a condition inside the if statement, it will be considered true only when all the elements in b satisfy the condition.

3. Update the position with this new value:

```
rnew=r+rstep;
```

After we are done with one time step, we can put a loop around it to make it an iterative process and let it run for, let us say, 1000 time steps. We initialize r as the origin before the first time step.

```
r=[0 0];
for t= 0:0.1:100
                b=rand(1,2);
                w=b>0.5;
                if w==1
                        rstep=[1 0];
                elseif w(1)==1
                        rstep=[0 1];
                elseif w(2)==1
                            rstep=[-1 0];
                else
                            rstep=[0 -1];
                end
        rnew=r+rstep;
        r=rnew;
end
```

Animation of the walk

Using the animation techniques learnt in previous chapters, we can also visualize the random walk by plotting each step as a line connecting the previous location to the new one.

```
plot([r(1) rnew(1)],[r(2) rnew(2)]);
```

Since we are adding each step to the previous trace, we need to use hold on at least once so that the previous steps are not deleted.

```
hold on;
plot([r(1) rnew(1)],[r(2) rnew(2)]);
drawnow
```

When we run this code, we will get Figure 5-3. We can increase the time limit by changing the for loop time vector.

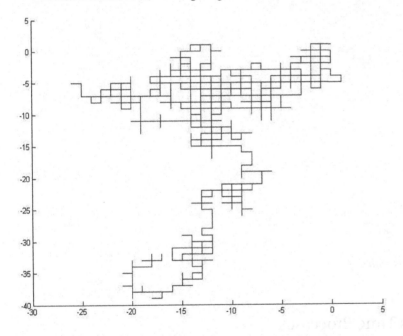

Figure 5-3. *Simulation of a random walk*

Adding Drift

In the plot you can see that, as time passes, the object starts to return to the origin. It never stays at the origin, but it has the tendency to move around the origin and the expected distance from the origin at $t=\infty$ is 0. This is because the selection of each direction is equally probable. For example, the probability that the [1 0] direction is chosen is given as

$$\Pr[Selected\ Direction = +X] = P[w_1 = 1\ \&\ w_2 = 1]$$
$$= P(w_1 = 1) \times P(w_2 = 1)$$
$$= P(b_1 > 0.5) P(b_2 > 0.5) = \frac{1}{4}$$

Now let us change the probabilities and observe its effect. We can change the direction selection step as follows:

```
b=rand(1,2);
w=b>[0.4 0.3];
```

Now we are comparing b1 with 0.4 and b2 with 0.3. So the probability of selecting the +X direction is given by

$$Pr[Selected\ Direction=+X]=P(b_1>0.4)P(b_2>0.3)=0.6\times0.7=0.42$$

and so forth. The result is shown in Figure 5-4. We can clearly see a tendency of the walk to move in the +XY directions. This illustrates the motion of the object when a drifting force exists in the medium.

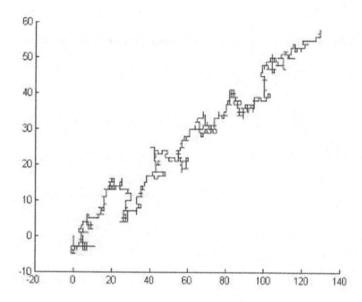

Figure 5-4. *Simulation of a random walk with drift*

Simulation of Continuous Time Processes

A continuous time process x(t) can again be represented mainly in two ways:

1. Explicit form, for example

$$x(t)=t\sin(t+\phi)+e^{-t}\cos(t)+w(t)$$

2. Time update equations

Here the rate of change of the process describes its dynamics. For example, consider a process x(t) defined by

$$\frac{dx(t)}{dt}=\cos t+2e^{-t}+0.4+w(t)$$

where w(t) is the input signal.

The first form is trivial, as before, so we concentrate on the second form. The first task when simulating such systems is to convert the system to a discrete time system via the following steps:

1. Fix a sample time interval δ and sample the system with time step δ

$$t = t_0 + \delta n$$

where t_0 is the start of the world, typically taken as 0.

2. Next replace the derivate terms by the first principle definition of differentiation

$$\frac{dx(t)}{dt} = \frac{x(t+\delta) - x(t)}{\delta}$$

Thus, using the sample time definition, $x(t+\delta)$ can be written as

$$x(t+\delta) = x(t_0 + \delta n + \delta) = x[n+1]$$

Let us work on the above mentioned example. The time update equation can be written as

$$\frac{x(t+\delta) - x(t)}{\delta} = \cos t + 2e^{-t} + 0.4 + w(t)$$

$$\frac{x[n+1] - x[n]}{\delta} = \cos \delta n + 2e^{-\delta n} + 0.4 + w[n]$$

$$x[n+1] = x[n] + \delta \left(\cos \delta n + 2e^{-\delta n} + 0.4 + w[n] \right)$$

which is in the same format as the discrete system discussed in the previous section and can be simulated in a similar way. We can actually save the whole process with respect to time instead of just keeping the current value. Recall that, in the previous example, at each step we updated r to rnew. At the end of the simulation, you don't have access to the locations at previous times. In the following code, we will save all the values in a matrix x where the nth element of the matrix represents x[n]. We also assume that the input w(t) is zero. (See Figure 5-5.)

```
x(1)=[0];
delta=0.1;
for i= 1:100
        x(i+1)=x(i)+delta*(cos(delta*i)+2*exp(-delta*i)+0.4);
end
plot(1:101,x);
```

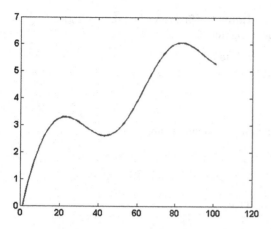

Figure 5-5. *Simulation of a continuous time process*

Let us now see how we can compute the motion of a projectile as discussed in the first section. At any time step, the update in velocity is given as

$$v_x[n+1]=v_x[n]$$
$$v_y[n+1]=v_y[n]-g\delta$$

and the location is updated as

$$x_x[n+1]=x_x[n]+v_x[n]\delta$$
$$x_y[n+1]=x_y[n]+v_y[n]\delta$$

The simulation should terminate when the ball hits the ground, i.e. when x_y is less than zero.

```
v=[10 20];g=9.8;x=[0 0];
delta=0.1;t=0;
while (x(2)>=0)
        v=v+[0 -g*delta];
        x=x+v*delta;
        plot(x(1),x(2),'ro','MarkerSize',6);
hold on;
axis([0 60 0 40])
drawnow;
t=t+delta;
end
flighttime=t;
range=x(1);
```

Example: Balls in a 2D Box

Let us consider a complex example. Suppose there are N balls in a 2D plane, given initial velocities and confined within some boundary $(-L \leq x, y \leq L)$. As the balls move in a plane, if they collide with other balls, they exchange their velocities and continue moving. If they hit the boundary, they reverse their component of velocity, which is in the direction of confinement. For example, if they hit x=L, their velocity will change as

$$v'_x = -v_x$$

$$v'_y = v_y$$

We are interested in simulating this system for two minutes with a time interval of 0.1s, which corresponds to 1200 time step evaluations as

$$N_t = \frac{T}{\delta} = \frac{120}{.1} = 1200$$

To simulate this, we follow the same procedure. First, let us fix the notation we are going to use in the MATLAB code. The x location of the ith ball at time n is going to be stored as bx(i,n). Similarly, we store the y location of the ith ball in by(i,n), the x component of the velocity of ball i at step n is stored in vx(i,n) and the y component in vy(i,n). Let us see what happens to a particular ball at time step n given the x locations and velocities of all balls at time step n.

1. Determine if the ball is hitting any other ball. A hit occurs if the distance between two balls is less than the sum of their radii. Let us assume that a ball can hit only one ball at any time, so if more than one ball satisfies the distance criteria, we will just take the closest of all such balls. If such a collision occurs, we set hit equal to 1.

```
Dis=(bx(i, n)-bx([1:i-1 i+1:end],n]).^2...
                          +(by(i, n)-by([1:i-1 i+1:end],n]).^2;
[closestDistance closestBall]=min(Dis);
%since we are now counting i, adjust the index of the closest ball % to reflect the true index
if closestBall>i-1
        closestBall=closestBall+1;
end
if closestDistance<(2*r)^2
        hit=1;
end
```

2. Determine if the ball has hit the wall. It is a hit if the ball is outside the boundary. In this case we set hit equal to 2.

```
if bx(i,n)>=L-r || bx(i,n)<=-L+r || by(i,n)>=L-r || by(i,n)<=-L+r
        hit =2;
end
```

3. If there is a hit, update the velocity at n+1 for the ith ball accordingly.

```
if hit==1
    vx(i,n+1)=vx(closestBall,n);
    vy(i,n+1)=vy(closestBall,n);
elseif hit==2
    vx(i,n+1)=vx(i,n);
```

```
                    vy(i,n+1)=vy(i,n);
                    if bx(i,n)>=L-r || bx(i,n)<=-L+r
                        vx(i,n+1)=-vx(i,n);
                    end
                    if by(i,n)>=L-r || by(i,n)<=-L+r
                        vy(i,n+1)=-vy(i,n);
                    end
                else
                    vx(i,n+1)=vx(i,n);
                    vy(i,n+1)=vy(i,n);
                end
```

4. Update the location for n+1 using the velocity at n+1.

```
    bx(i,n+1)=bx(i,n)+delta*vx(i,n+1);
    by(i,n+1)=by(i,n)+delta*vy(i,n+1);
```

Having carried out all the above steps, we obtain the velocity and location of ball *i* for time step n+1. Now we need to do the above for all the balls and then repeat it for each time step.

Animation

Now we can visualize the motion of the balls by plotting each individual ball as a circle inside the 2D boundary. The following code does the same:

```
clf; %clear the figure
%plot the boundary
plot([L -L -L L L],[L L -L -L L],'LineWidth',3);
hold on;
%create x and y for plotting a circle
theta=0:.1:2*pi;x=r*cos(theta);y=r*sin(theta);
%loop for all the balls
for i=1:N
        plot(bx(i,n)+x,by(i,n)+y,'LineWidth',4);
end
axis([-L-5 L+5 -L-5 L+5])
drawnow
```

The complete code will look something like the following:

```
r= r=0.2;
delta=0.1;n=0;N=7;L=10;
%initilialize
bx=L*(rand(N,1)-0.5);
by=L*(rand(N,1)-0.5);
vx=4*(rand(N,1)-0.5);
vy=4*(rand(N,1)-0.5);
%colors of balls
c='rgbcmyk';
for t=0:delta:120
    n=n+1;
```

```
for i=1:N
    hit=0;
    %computing the hits
    Dis=(bx(i, n)-bx([1:i-1 i+1:end],n)).^2 ...
    +(by(i, n)-by([1:i-1 i+1:end],n)).^2;
    [closestDistance closestBall]=min(Dis);
    if closestBall>i-1
        closestBall=closestBall+1;
    end
    if closestDistance<(2*r)^2
        hit=1;
    end
    if bx(i,n)>=L-r || bx(i,n)<=-L+r ...
                        || by(i,n)>=L-r || by(i,n)<=-L+r
        hit=2;
    end
    %updating velocities
    if hit==1
        vx(i,n+1)=vx(closestBall,n);
        vy(i,n+1)=vy(closestBall,n);
    elseif hit==2
        vx(i,n+1)=vx(i,n);
        vy(i,n+1)=vy(i,n);
        if bx(i,n)>=L-r || bx(i,n)<=-L+r
            vx(i,n+1)=-vx(i,n);
        end
        if by(i,n)>=L-r || by(i,n)<=-L+r
            vy(i,n+1)=-vy(i,n);
        end
    else
        vx(i,n+1)=vx(i,n);
        vy(i,n+1)=vy(i,n);
    end
    %updating the locations
    bx(i,n+1)=bx(i,n)+delta*vx(i,n+1);
    by(i,n+1)=by(i,n)+delta*vy(i,n+1);
end
%plotting
clf; %clear the figure
%plot the boundary
plot([L -L -L L L],[L L -L -L L],'LineWidth',3);
hold on;
%create x and y for plotting a circle
theta=0:.1:2*pi;x=r*cos(theta);y=r*sin(theta);
%loop for all the balls
for i=1:N
    plot(bx(i,n)+x,by(i,n)+y,c(i),'LineWidth',4);
end
axis([-L-5 L+5 -L-5 L+5])
drawnow
end
```

The above code will result in an animation, one frame of which will look like Figure 5-6.

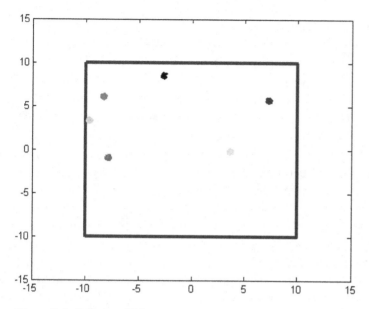

Figure 5-6. *Balls in a 2D box*

The above simulation has some issues and can be refined. For example, after each update of location, the locations can be checked for consistency so that no ball is beyond the boundary and no two balls intersect each other. In that case, the velocities and locations can be updated in the middle of the step by computing the time of hit and interpolating that way instead of waiting for the next time step to update. Let us also analyze the effect of the time step. As we decrease the time step, the simulation becomes more accurate as it is able to compute the hits more accurately. We can observe the impact of δ in the accuracy and continuity of the plots.

Motion in a Force Field

Let us assume that there are two force fields acting on each ball:

1.   An electrical force field of E which exerts a force of qE where q is the charge on each ball. The acceleration caused at each ball is $a_E = \dfrac{qE}{m}$ where m is the mass of each ball. We assume that odd numbered balls are positively charged while even numbered balls are negatively charged.

     ```
     q=1.6e-7*ones(N,1);q(2:2:end)=-1.6e-7;E=[1e6 0];m=1;
     ```

2.   There is a continuous flow of wind which causes the balls to drift in the direction of the wind, which applies an acceleration equal to a_w.

     ```
     aw=[.02 .02];
     ```

These forces will add a $(a_w + a_E)\delta$ term to the velocity at each time step. The rest of the code will be the same and only the updates of velocities will be modified as follows

```
%updating velocities
if hit==1
                        vx(i,n+1)=vx(closestBall,n);
                        vy(i,n+1)=vy(closestBall,n);
                    elseif hit==2
                        vx(i,n+1)=vx(i,n);
                        vy(i,n+1)=vy(i,n);
                        if bx(i,n)>=L-r || bx(i,n)<=-L+r
                                vx(i,n+1)=-vx(i,n);
                        end
                        if by(i,n)>=L-r || by(i,n)<=-L+r
                                vy(i,n+1)=-vy(i,n);
                        end
                    else
                        vx(i,n+1)=vx(i,n);
                        vy(i,n+1)=vy(i,n);
                    end
                    vx(i,n+1)=vx(i,n+1)+q(i)*E(1)/m*delta+aw(1)*delta;
        vy(i,n+1)=vy(i,n+1)+q(i)*E(2)/m*delta+aw(2)*delta;
```

Since there are drifts in the direction of the X axis, we need to verify the consistency of location at the end of the full iteration.

```
%updating the locations
bx(i,n+1)=bx(i,n)+delta*vx(i,n+1);
by(i,n+1)=by(i,n)+delta*vy(i,n+1);

%check consistancy
if bx(i,n+1)>L-r
    bx(i,n+1)=L-r;
end
if bx(i,n+1)<-L+r
    bx(i,n+1)=-L+r;
end
if by(i,n+1)>L-r
    by(i,n+1)=L-r;
end
if by(i,n+1)<-L+r
    by(i,n+1)=-L+r;
end
```

Let us plot the x location of ball 1 and 2 (see Figure 5-7).

```
plot((0:n)*delta,bx(1,:),'r','LineWidth',2)
hold on;
plot((0:n)*delta,bx(2,:),'g','LineWidth',2)
```

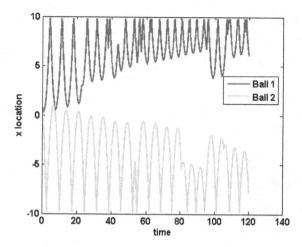

Figure 5-7. *Simulated path (x axis only) for balls 1 and 2 in force fields*

Event-based Simulations

We have seen how a continuous process can be converted to a discrete time process by sampling it with equal sample intervals. However, sometimes, updates of states don't happen at equal intervals $\{n\delta : n \in \mathbb{N}\}$ but instead these updates are determined by events $\{t_n : n \in \mathbb{N}\}$. For example, in the example from the previous section, velocities need not be updated at each sample time step, they are only updated after collisions with other balls and the wall. The obvious benefit of an event-based simulation is that it reduces the computation time as the events are sparse and there are significantly fewer events than time steps. Moreover, they affect the accuracy of the simulations too. For example, in the previous section, the collision may happen in the middle of the step. In that case, the simulation has to wait for the next time step before updating the velocities and, in this time, a ball will go inside the colliding ball in the simulation, which will never happen in the real world. Event-based simulations require computations of the times when events will happen well ahead of time and modelling the dynamics of the system to compute the updates of states. Consider the following process:

$$\frac{d}{dt}x(t) = f(t).$$

For a fixed interval simulation, x(t) is discretized as

$$x[n] = x(n\delta)$$

and we can easily compute the $x(t)$ at the next time step as

$$x[n+1] = x[n] + f(n\delta)\delta$$

if δ is small enough, whereas for the event-based simulation, x(t) is discretized as

$$x[n] = x(t_n)$$

and the value of x(t) at the next event needs to be computed as

$$x[n+1] = x[n] + \int_{t_n}^{t_{n+1}} f(t)\,dt.$$

Let us take a simple example of a bouncing ball. Suppose a ball with elasticity constant e is dropped at velocity 0 from height h. The ball hits the ground with some velocity v and bounces back into the air with velocity $v_{1b}=-v$. It then goes up and comes back again to hit the ground with velocity v_{1e} and bounces back with velocity $v_{2b}=-ev_{1e}$. From the symmetry of flight we know that $v_{ib}=v_{ie}$ for the ith bounce. Here each bounce is an event. Note that the velocity and locations are still changing continuously between events and we need to compute the ball's motion until the next event ahead of time at the previous event itself. We know that at the ith bounce, the location of the ball is given by

$$h(t)=v_{ib}\left(t-t_i\right)-\frac{1}{2}g\left(t-t_i\right)^2$$

where t_i is the start of the ith bounce. Let us simulate the system for n bounces (see Figure 5-8).

```
u=0;g=9.8;H=20;e=0.7;n=10;
%time until first bounce
T=sqrt(2*H/g);v=-g*T;vb(1)=-e*v;t(1)=T;
tempt=0:T/20:T;
temph=H+u*tempt-0.5*g*(tempt).^2;
plot(tempt,temph,'b','Linewidth',2);
%color for each bounce
c='rgbcmykrgbcmykrgbcmyk';
hold on;
for i=1:n
        ve(i)=-vb(i);       %speed at the end of the ith bounce
        vb(i+1)=-e*ve(i); %speed at the beginning of the i+1th bounce
        ft(i)=2*vb(i)/g;    %flight time of ith bounce.
        h(i)=0.5*g*(ft(i)/2)^2; %height achieved in the ith bounce
        t(i+1)=t(i)+ft(i); %start of the i+1 bounce
        %computation for the ith bounce
        tempt=t(i):ft(i)/20:t(i+1);
        temph=vb(i)*(tempt-t(i))-0.5*g*((tempt-t(i))).^2;
        %plot the ith bounce
        plot(tempt,temph,c(i),'Linewidth',2);
end
```

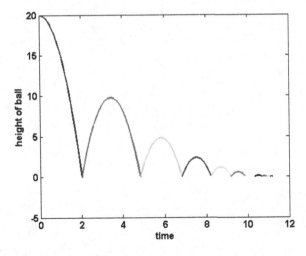

Figure 5-8. *Simulated motion of a bouncing ball*

For the next example, we will learn how we can simulate a birth-death process $x(t)$. Suppose there is a bus ticket counter queue where the customers' arrivals are independent Poisson arrivals, which means that the time until the next customer arrives is exponential with parameter λ and is independent of everything else. Also assume that each customer first waits for his turn to come to the counter in a queue and, once he is at the counter, the bus representative takes time T to issue the ticket. T is again an exponentially distributed random variable with parameter μ independent of everything else. Assume the first come first served policy. Here there are two types of events:

1. Birth, which is the arrival of a customer.

2. Death, which is the departure of a customer.

Whenever an event happens, we need to update the system and also compute the time and type of the next event and then move the simulation ahead to that time. Let us assume that Q denotes the number of customers waiting in the room, including the person at the service counter. Let us first concentrate on one step where one event has just happened:

1. If the type is death, reduce Q by 1 if Q>0, else increase Q by 1.

```
if type(i)==1
        Q(i+1)=Q(i)-1*(Q(i)>0);
else
        Q(i+1)=Q(i)+1;
end
```

2. Compute the next event and the event time. For this, generate two random variables $A \sim exp(\lambda)$ and $B \sim exp(\mu)$ and take the minimum of the two. If A is the minimum, the next event is an arrival, otherwise it will be a departure and the time of the next event will be that minimum value.

```
A=exprnd(lambda);B=exprnd(mu);
[nexttime type(i+1)]=min([A B]);
T(i+1)=T(i)+nexttime;
```

Now we can iterate the steps and plot Q (see Figure 5-9).

```
lambda=0.9;
mu=1;
type=[0 2];
Q=0;
T=[0 exprnd(lambda)];
for i=2:50
if type(i)==1
        Q(i)=Q(i-1)-1*(Q(i-1)>0);
else
Q(i)=Q(i-1)+1;
end
A=exprnd(lambda);B=exprnd(mu);
[nexttime type(i+1)]=min([A B]);
T(i+1)=T(i)+nexttime;
end
stairs(T(1:end-1),Q,'LineWidth',2)
createfigure('time','Q');
```

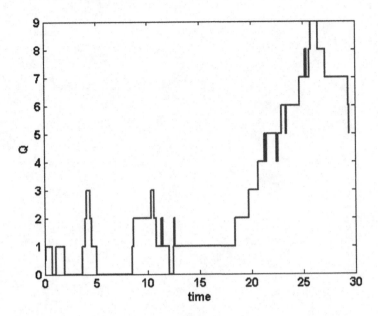

Figure 5-9. *A realization of a birth-death process*

■ ■ ■

CHAPTER 6

Monte Carlo Simulations

Most real world processes have some random components in them. That is why we have to investigate the statistical properties of such systems/processes. For example, we may be interested in computing the expected performance of a system or the expected distance in a random walk process, or the mean power of a received signal or the expected number of people in a waiting room (see the last example in Chapter 5). Many mathematical tools have been derived to compute such metrics, however in most cases the systems are too complex to derive any tractable results. In such scenarios, simulations with random sampling, also known as Monte Carlo simulations, can provide the desired analysis. This technique is based on the assumption that if we perform random sampling of a random variable sufficiently many times, we can derive the approximate statistical properties of it. On the other hand, we sometimes add the random component into a computation or algorithm deliberately when deterministic computation is very extensive or difficult. Monte Carlo simulations are also very useful in such cases.

Random Sampling

In this section, we will discuss the basic concept behind Monte Carlo simulation and see why it achieves the almost-correct solution. Let us start with a simple example of computing the third moment of a Gaussian random variable.

The Third Moment of a Gaussian Random Variable

Suppose X is a Gaussian random variable with mean m and variance s. Suppose we want to compute the third moment of such a random variable. We know that the distribution of a Gaussian random variable is given by

$$f(x) = \frac{1}{\sqrt{2\pi s}} e^{-\frac{1}{2}\frac{(x-m)^2}{s}}$$

and the third moment is given by

$$E\left[X^3\right] = \int_{-\infty}^{\infty} x^3 f(x)\,dx$$

which we can compute via the following code

```
h=.01;
m=1;s=1;
x=-10:h:10+m;
y=x.^3.*1/sqrt(2*pi*s)*exp(-0.5*(x-m).^2/s);
mom3_int=trapz(x,y);
```

69

Here the accuracy of the code is dependent on the value of h and the range of computation (which is -10:10 here). Let us see how we can compute the third moment using Monte Carlo simulation. We know that the sample third moment is given by

$$E\left[X^3\right]=\frac{1}{N}\sum_{n=1:N}x_n^3$$

where x is sampled from the given distribution $X \sim N(m,s)$. The following code implements the above computation:

```
N=10000;
x=m+sqrt(s)*randn(N,1);
mom3_sam=sum(x.^3)/N;
```

Here the accuracy is given by the value of N. As we increase N, the error drops as $1/\sqrt{N}$. We compare the values of both terms (mom3_int=4, mom3_sam=4.04). The latter simulation is known as a Monte Carlo simulation because random sampling is used to compute the metric.

Moments of Random Processes

Similarly we can compute the statistical properties of any random process. Consider the following random process

$$y(t)=\sin(t+\phi)+w(t)$$

where w(t) is the additive Gaussian random noise with unit variance and zero mean and ϕ is a uniform random variable $U[0,2\pi]$. Suppose that we are interested in finding the mean $E[y(t)]$ of this process at time $t = t_0$. There are three approaches to solving this problem.

Sampling Realizations of the Process

We can generate multiple realizations of the process and collect one sample y(t) from each realization at some fixed time $t = t_0$ and then compute the mean of all these samples.

```
t0=4;sampletime=0.01;t=0:sampletime:10;
for i=1:1000
        phi=rand(1)*pi*2;
        w=randn(size(t));
        y=sin(t+phi)+w;
        samplesyatt0(i)=y(t0/sampletime+1);
end
meanatt0=mean(samplesyatt0);
```

Time Averaging

Since we know that the process is stationary and ergodic, $E[y(t)]$ will be independent of the time t and can also be computed using time averaging by the following equation

$$E\left[y(t)\right]=\frac{1}{T}\int_0^T y(t)\,dt$$

```
t0=4;sampletime=0.01;t=0:sampletime:10;
phi=rand(1)*pi*2;
w=randn(size(t));
y=sin(t+phi)+w;
meanatt=1/10*trapz(t,y);
```

Time Sampling

We can also compute the mean of $x(t)$ by taking samples of just one realization of the process at uniform time intervals and then computing the mean of all these samples.

```
t0=4;sampletime=0.01;t=0:sampletime:10;
phi=rand(1)*pi*2;
w=randn(size(t));
y=sin(t+phi)+w;
meanatt=mean(y);
```

Sampling from a Given Distribution

We will see that almost all the methods used in this chapter will need random values generated from some given distribution in order to compute results. Therefore it is essential to first learn how we can sample a distribution to generate random values from it.

Inbuilt Functions

MATLAB provides inbuilt functions for the generation of random samples from many standard distributions. Here are a few examples.

Uniform Distribution

```
U=rand(N,M);
%Generates an NxM vector of U(0,1)
```

```
U=a+(b-a)*rand(N,M);
%Generates an NxM vector of U(a,b)
```

Gaussian Distribution

```
X=randn(N,M);
%Generates an NxM vector of N(0,1)
```

```
X=m+sqrt(s)*rand(N,M);
%Generates an NxM vector of N(m,s)
```

Exponential Distribution

```
X=exprnd(m,N,M);
%Generates NxM vector of Exp(m)
```

Bernoulli Distribution

```
p=0.3;
U=rand(N,M)<p;
```

Rejection Sampling

Rejection sampling is a basic technique used to generate observations from an arbitrary distribution. Suppose we want to sample X where X follows the probability distribution function $f(x)$ and there are no inbuilt functions for sampling from $f(x)$. Let us take another distribution function $g(x)$ such that sampling from $g(x)$ is easy. (If we have many choices for $g(x)$, we prefer the one which looks similar to $f(x)$). We first compute the envelope

$$M = sup \frac{f(x)}{g(x)}$$

so that

$$f(x) < Mg(x).$$

Now we perform the rejection sampling algorithm as follows:

1. Sample x from $g(x)$ and u from $U(0,1)$.

2. Check whether $u<f(x)/Mg(x)$ or not.

3. If this holds, accept x as a realization of f(x).

4. If not, reject the value of x and repeat the sampling step.

The accepted samples will be from $f(x)$ Let us consider a sample implementation of the algorithm. Suppose we want to sample from the pdf shown in Figure 6-1.

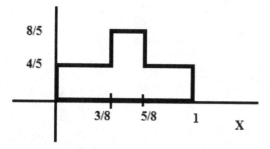

Figure 6-1. *f(x)*

Let us choose the uniform distribution as g(x). We see that we can choose M=8/5 since $f(x) < \frac{8}{5}g(x)$. The following code implements the rejection sampling:

```
M=8/5;N=10000;
f=@(x) 4/5*((x>0 & x<1)+(x>3/8&x<5/8));
g=@(x) (x<1 & x>0);
xsamples=[];
```

```
for i=1:N
        u=rand(1);
        x=rand(1);
        if u<f(x)/(M*g(x))
                xsamples=[xsamples x];
        end
end
hist(xsamples);
```

We can also implement the same algorithm using vectorization. We can sample N number of *u*s and *x*s and accept or reject them in one shot.

```
u=rand(N,1);x=rand(N,1);
accept=u<f(x)./(M*g(x));
xsamples=x(accept);
hist(xsamples)
```

The histogram of the sample will appear as shown in Figure 6-2, which confirms that these are samples from *f*(*x*)

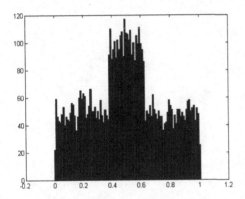

Figure 6-2. *Histogram of f(x) obtained using rejection sampling*

Gibbs Sampling

Sampling of random variables becomes harder as we move to multivariate distributions. Since there are very few inbuilt sampling functions for multivariate distributions in MATLAB, we will discuss a very simple but elegant algorithm known as Gibbs sampling used for this purpose (Figure 6-3).

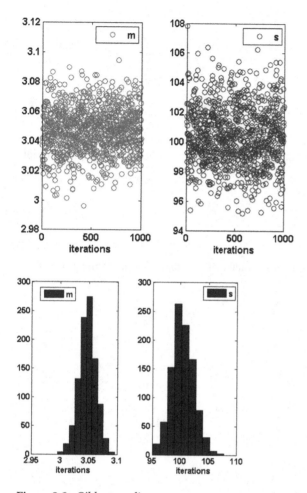

Figure 6-3. *Gibbs sampling*

The idea is to represent the multivariate distribution as a combination of conditional probability distributions of each variable and them sample from these single variable distribution one at a time, conditioned on the current values of other random variables. For example, consider the posterior distribution of the mean and variance of a normal data set $\{x_i\}$ which is given by

$$p(m,s) = G \frac{1}{s^{a+1}} exp\left(-\frac{2b+l(m-m')^2}{2s}\right)$$

$$a = \alpha + \frac{n}{2} + \frac{1}{2}$$

$$b = \beta + \frac{1}{2}l(m-m')^2 + \frac{1}{2}\left[\sum(x_i)^2 + \lambda\mu^2 - \frac{\left(\sum x_i + \lambda\mu\right)^2}{n+\lambda}\right]$$

$$l = n + \lambda$$

$$m' = \frac{\sum x_i + \lambda\mu}{n+\lambda}$$

As the joint distribution is very complicated, it is hard to sample directly from this distribution. But we can see that conditional distribution $p(m|s)$ and $p(s|m)$ are given as

$$p(m|s) = N\left(m', \frac{s}{l}\right)$$

$$p(s|m) = IG(a, b)$$

which are easy to sample. However, note that we need the value of s for $p(m|s)$ and the value of m for $p(s|m)$. The Gibbs sampling suggests we take some value of m and sample s from p(s|m). and then use this sample s to sample m from $p(m|s)$ and so on. The final algorithm is given as:

1. Take an initial value m_0.

2. Sample $s_1 \sim IG\left(\alpha + \frac{n}{2} + \frac{1}{2}, \beta + \frac{1}{2}l(m - m')^2 + \frac{1}{2}\left[\sum(x_i)^2 + \lambda\mu^2 - \frac{\left(\sum x_i + \lambda\mu\right)^2}{n + \lambda}\right]\right)$.

3. Sample $m_1 \sim N\left(\dfrac{\sum x_i + \lambda\mu}{n + \lambda}, \dfrac{s_1}{n + \lambda}\right)$.

4. Take $m_0 = m_1$ and repeat step 1.

The steps of Gibbs sampling can be implemented easily. First, we need the data x which is generally given to us from some experiment. For this example, we generate a dummy data x:

```
n=5000;x=3+10randn(n,1);
```

Then the rest of the algorithm can be implemented as

```
%parameters
par_mu=0.3;par_lambda=10;par_alpha=1;par_beta=1;
%initilize value of m
m_0=0.3;
%perform conditional sampling
for i=1:1000
        l=n+par_lambda;
        mprime=(sum(x)+par_lambda*par_mu)/(n+par_lambda);
                        a=par_alpha+n/2+1/2;
        b=par_beta+1/2*l*(m_0-mprime)^2 ...
                +1/2*[sum(x.^2)+par_lambda*par_mu^2-...
 (sum(x)+par_lambda*par_mu)^2/(n+par_lambda)];
        s_1=1/gamrnd(a,1/b);
        m_1= mprime+randn(1)* sqrt(s1/(n+par_lambda));
        M(i)=m_1;
        S(i)=s_1;
        m_0=m_1;
end

%plot the samples
subplot(1,2,1);plot(M,'ro ');legend('m');
subplot(1,2,2);plot(S,'bo ');legend('s');
```

```
%plot sample distribution
figure
subplot(1,2,1);hist(M);
legend('m');
subplot(1,2,2);hist(S);
legend('s');
```

Gibbs sampling is a special case of a broader class of computational algorithms known as Markov Chain Monte Carlo (MCMC) algorithms. In this class of algorithms, we generate a chain of random samples where each sample is dependent on the previous sample (hence the name Markov chain). Note that the initial sample is arbitrarily chosen by us. In general practice, the implementation should wait for some time and then start collecting the samples. This waiting time should be enough to let the chain settle and produce independent samples. This waiting time is known as the burn-in time and depends on the complexity of the Markov chain.

Statistical Performance

As discussed, the primary use of Monte Carlo simulation is to compute statistical properties, such as expected performance of systems/processes. In this section, we will see a few more examples of how we can evaluate the statistical performance of a given system/process.

Computation of pi

We know the ratio of the area of the shaded disc to the square in Figure 6-4 is $\frac{\pi}{4}$. We also know that if we select a point randomly over the area of the square, the probability that it will fall inside the circle will be proportional to the area of circle, therefore it will be equal to the ratio $\frac{\pi}{4}$.

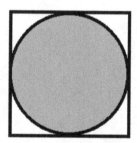

Figure 6-4. Computation of pi

Now, using the random sampling argument, we can say that if we select N points in the square, the number of points falling inside the circle will be approximately $\pi N/4$. Therefore we can compute the value of π by simulating this sampling using the following code:

```
N=1000;
X=rand(N,2)-1/2;
Dis=sqrt(sum(X.^2,2));
Ncircle=sum(Dis<1/2);
Pi_sam=4*Ncircle/N;
```

Communication Channels

Monte Carlo simulation is widely used in communications to evaluate wireless systems. In this section, we will discuss one specific channel model and see how we can compute its performance using a Monte Carlo method.

Consider a transmitter (Tx)-receiver (Rx) pair where Tx transmits a signal x[n] which is a Bernoulli random variable with $p = \frac{1}{2}$. The signal is received at Rx after being attenuated by the channel according to the following equation

$$y[n] = h[n]x[n] + w[n]$$

where h[n] is Rayleigh distributed and w[n] is Gaussian noise $N(0,\sigma^2)$. Let the decoder output be $\hat{x}[n]$. Since y[n] is a real value, the receiver decodes the original message by comparing y[n] with 0 and decoding y[n] as 1 if $y[n] \geq 0$. An error happens if $\hat{x}[n]$ is not equal to y[n]. Our goal is to evaluate the average rate of error which is defined as the ratio between the total number of errors and the total number of transmissions. This is also known as the probability of error.

```
N=1000;
%generate the transmitted signal
x=rand(N,1)>0.5;
%channel
h=sqrt(sum(1/sqrt(2)*randn(N,2).^2,2));
sigmasq=0.1;
w=randn(N,1)*sqrt(sigmasq);
%add noise and fading
y=h.*x+w;
%decode
yd=y>0;
e=abs(x-yd)>0;
ProbError=sum(e)/N;
```

Birth-Death Processes

Now let us consider the birth-death process discussed in the previous chapter. Suppose the station manager is interested in finding the expected number of customers in the queue so that he can put enough chairs in the waiting room.

As we have seen in previous examples, we can compute the value by running the birth-death process many times and taking one sample of the number of waiting customers at some fixed time (sufficiently long after burn-in to let the chain settle) and compute the mean of these samples. But we can also use only one realization of the process. The idea is to run the same birth-death process for a long time and collect the values for the number of waiting customers in the room at uniform time samples and then compute the mean of these values. The results from both simulations will be the same as this chain is ergodic and averaging across time will give the same result as averaging across different realizations. The second approach is efficient as it uses only one realization. Let us assume we have run the code given in the previous chapter and we have obtained the matrices t and q containing all time events and the number of waiting customers at those time events. The following code computes the mean number of waiting customers in the room.

```
T_sample=0.1;
Time=0:T_sample:t(end-1);
X=zeros(size(Time));
for i=1:length(t)-1
        X(t(i)<Time & Time<t(i+1))=q(i);
end
meanwait=mean(X);
```

Multidimensional Integrals

In the first section, we saw that we need to solve an integral to compute the moment of a random variable and, with the help of a Monte Carlo simulation, we can convert this problem to a sampling problem which avoids any integration step. Now we can extend this idea to compute any integral using a Monte Carlo method, which is very helpful for multidimensional integration.

Let us consider the following example where we have to compute the integral

$$I = \int_0^\infty sin(x) exp(-2x) dx.$$

Observe that if we take

$$p(x) = 2exp(-2x),$$

then we can write the above integral as

$$I = \int_0^\infty \frac{1}{2} sin(x) p(x) dx.$$

Since $p(x)$ is equal to the probability distribution function $p_Y(y)$ of an exponential random variable Y given as

$$p_Y(y) = 2exp(-2y)1(y \geq 0),$$

the integral can also be seen as the following expectation

$$I = \frac{1}{2} E[sin(Y)] = \int_0^\infty \frac{1}{2} sin(y) p_Y(y) dy,$$

which can be computed using a Monte Carlo method. Note that the initial integral has no random variable in it, but we created a dummy random variable Y and represented the expression in the form of an expectation term. Let us compare both computations

```
%Integration
x=[0:.01:100];
y=sin(x).*exp(-2*x);
I_i==trapz(x,y);

%random sampling
Y=exprnd(2,10000,1);
I_s=mean(0.5*sin(Y));
```

We get $I_i = 0.2$, $I_s = 0.1955$.

There is another way to approach this integral computation problem. We can use the approach used to compute π in the previous section. Let us consider the following example

$$I = \int_0^{10} sin(x) exp(-x) dx.$$

Since the integral I also denotes the area under the curve sin(x)exp(-2x) (see Figure 6-5), to compute this area, we can randomly sample points in the square area A and count the number the points under the curve. Then the ratio of the number of points inside the curve to the number of total points should be equal to ratio of areas.

$$\frac{A_c}{A} = \frac{N_c}{N} \rightarrow A_c = \frac{N_c}{N}A$$

```
N=1000;
A=0.40*10;
X=10*rand(N,1);
Y=.40*rand(N,1)-.05;
Fx=sin(X).*exp(-X);
Ncurve=sum(Fx<Y);
I_a=A*Ncurve/N;
```

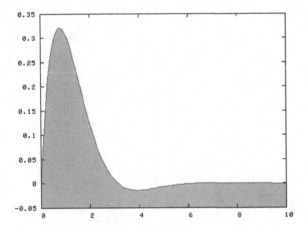

Figure 6-5. *Monte Carlo for integration*

Now let us consider a multi-dimensional integral. As we have seen earlier, the first step in numerical integration is to generate a grid. As the dimension d increases, the grid size increases as n^d where n is the size of a one dimensional grid. We can see that the grid becomes significantly large very quickly with d, causing MATLAB to throw an out of memory error. Hence an integral cannot be computed using this approach whereas Monte Carlo simulation can still be run as it can generate the random samples one at a time or by blocks. Also the error variance in a Monte Carlo method goes as $\frac{1}{N}$ where N is the number of iterations, which is independent of the number of dimensions. Consider the following example

$$I = \int_0^1\int_0^1 sin\left(2\pi\left(x+y\right)\right)dx\,dy$$

which can be represented as the following quantity

$$I_e = E\left[sin2\pi(X+Y)\right]$$

where $X, Y \sim U(0,1)$ and are independent of each other. Therefore the integral can be computed by the following code.

```
X=rand(1000,1);
Y=rand(1000,1);
z=sin(2*pi*(X+Y));
I_e=mean(z);
```

Summary

In this chapter, we learnt how to simulate a system with random components and how to compute its statistical properties and performance using Monte Carlo methods. We have also seen how we can sample random variables from any given distribution using MCMC methods. We recommend the reader to find out more about other MCMC methods such as the Metropolis Hasting algorithm, importance sampling, particle filtering etc. We also learnt how we can use Monte Carlo methods to evaluate multidimensional integrals.

■ ■ ■

CHAPTER 7

Optimization

An important aspect of any engineering design problem is to achieve efficiency. This can be in terms of energy consumption, performance, time complexity, etc. In many cases, we have multiple solutions to a problem and we have to select the most efficient solution. Finding the optimal solution from all the available options is known as optimization. Optimization plays an important role in various engineering applications such as design optimization, transportation, computation, manufacturing, economics and game theory. There is a broad body of work involving the mathematical theories behind optimization, aimed at designing efficient algorithms. In this chapter, we will concentrate on the implementation of numerical methods for optimization.

Optimization Overview

We will first briefly discuss the main aspects of an optimization problem and how to build a mathematical model for it. Let us consider an important real world problem in transportation. Commuting is big part of our lives and every day we have to travel several miles to go to work, home or to complete other personal/professional activities. So of course we would like to save as much time as we can. Can we just choose the shortest path to travel? The answer is no, as the shortest path may have a higher volume of traffic. Then what should be the optimal path? To find the answer, we would model the problem as an optimization problem and attempt to choose the best path.

The Optimization Goal

The prime objective that we want to maximize or minimize is known as the objective function or optimization goal. In the example we considered, the objective is to minimize the time taken to travel from point A (let us say Austin, TX) to point B (Houston, TX).

Design Parameters

The optimization goal can be dependent on many parameters. In this example, the time taken will be dependent on the path taken (e.g. its length, elevation and road conditions), the journey time (which defines the traffic), environmental conditions and vehicle or mode of transportation (for example, should I choose bus, car or bike? Sometimes it is faster to go by bike than by car for short distances if parking can cause delays). These parameters can be further dependent on/consist of other parameters, e.g. vehicle parameters consist of mileage, vehicle conditions, and so on. The parameters may also be dependent on each other, e.g. a vehicle's performance is dependent on elevation of path taken.

Constraints

There may be constraints while selecting the optimal path. For example, to go from Austin to Houston we can always take a flight to save time, but it may not be within our budget. We may want to choose a path which costs less than a fixed amount, say $50. Other constraints may be on our travel time, for example we can't go to an office at night even if the traffic is lowest at night.

The Optimization Domain

The optimization domain defines the set of all possible values we can select. It is a kind of direct constraint on parameters. It can be a continuous or discrete range, finite or infinite. For example, we may have only three or four paths available for travelling and we have to select one. The time of the journey may range only from 7am-9am. Also, we may have only four types of vehicle options.

The Optimization Problem

Now once we have seen all aspects of an optimization problem, we can formally define the problem as the following:

$$\frac{minimize}{path,\ time\ of\ the\ day,\ mode\ of\ transportation,\ vehicle}\ time$$

Mathematical Approach

Now we can formally describe a mathematical model of the problem. As discussed before, an optimization is performed to find the design parameters, $x = \{x_1, x_2, \ldots, x_n\}$, such that it can minimize the cost $C(x)$ or maximize the performance $P(x)$ which is dependent on x. The general problem can be stated as

$$\min_x f(x)$$

subject to

$$G_i(x) = 0 \ for\ i = 1, 2, \ldots, l$$
$$G_i(x) \le 0 \ for\ i = l, l+1, \ldots, n$$

where x is the vector design parameters of length n, f(x) is the objective function (equal to $C(x)$ or $-P(x)$) which returns a scalar value, and the vector function G(x) returns a vector of length n containing the values of the equality and inequality constraints evaluated at x. For the current example, the design parameters x can be represented as a vector

$$x = [P, T\_start, traportation\_medium, vehicle\_type]$$

and the optimal travel time problem can be written as

$$\min_x t(x)$$

such that

$$T\_start \in [7am - 9am]$$

$$transport\_medium \in \{bus, plane, car\}$$

$$vehicle\_type \in [2\,seater\,car,\ three\ seater\,car]$$

$$cost(transport\_medium, vehicle\_type) \leq \$50$$

Implementation

In this section, we will see how we can numerically solve an optimization problem by implementing a few optimization algorithms. There are many optimization methods currently available, but we will discuss only the extensive search and gradient descent methods as the other methods can be implemented similarly. Consider the minimization of the following function:

$$f(x) = x^2 + \cos(4x)$$

Extensive Search

One way to find the minimum value is by observation. Let us plot the function first to observe its behavior in the range [0:1]:

```
x=[0:0.01:1];f=@(x) x.^2+cos(4*x);
y=f(x);
plot(x,y);
```

From this, it can observed that there seems to be a minimum value near 0.6. To find the exact value we can call the min function

```
[foptvalue xoptin]=min(y);
xopt=x(xoptin);
```

which gives us the value xopt = 0.7. Since the step size is 0.01, the answer will be significant only to two digits. To get a more accurate solution, we can zoom in near the xopt value with a smaller step size and repeat the previous step

```
x=xopt+[-0.1:.001:0.1];
y=f(x);
plot(x,y);
[foptvalue xoptin]=min(y);
xopt=x(xoptin);
```

which gives the answer xopt=0.6960, which is exact to three decimal places. We can again repeat the same process by taking the step size .0001 and zooming to the current point. Note that we can choose the step size to be .0001 in the first step itself, but it would cause the search space grid to be very large and may result in a slower computation or an out of memory error. We can also automate the repetition by using a while loop.

```
xopt=0.5;stepsize=.05;
while stepsize>1e-5
                x=xopt+stepsize*[-10:1:10];
                y=f(x);
                plot(x,y);
                drawnow;
                [foptvalue xoptin]=min(y);
                xopt=x(xoptin);
                disp(xopt);
                stepsize=stepsize/10;
end
```

The Gradient Descent Method

Gradient descent is one of the most widely used methods to solve a convex optimization problem. In this iterative algorithm, we start from an initial point x_0 and step towards the direction of negative gradient (where the function is decreasing) at each iteration. The size of each step is proportional to the value of the gradient at the current x value at that iteration. Using this method, we can hope to reach local minima as we are always moving in the direction of the function decrease.

Let us suppose we are interested in minimizing the function f(x) and we start from an initial guess x_0. Then the step should be proportional to $-\nabla f(x_0)$ and the value for the next iteration should be given as

$$x_1 = x_0 - \gamma \nabla f(x_0)$$

where γ is the proportional constant and should be small enough to scan the values near local minima. Let us now implement the algorithm for our example case. The derivative of the function is given as

$$f'(x) = 2x - 4\sin(4x)$$

The following code implements the gradient descent method for the function f(x)

```
x_0=0.1;
f=@(x) x.^2+cos(4*x);
fprime=@(x) 2*x-4*sin(4*x);
tolerance=1e-5;
err_step=100;
g=.1;
while(err_step>tolerance)
        x_1=x_0-g*fprime(x_0);
        err_step=abs(x_1-x_0);
        x_0=x_1;
end
final_sol=x_1;
```

Compare the number of iterations taken to achieve the same accuracy.

Built-in Functions in MATLAB

There are many types of optimization problems and different algorithms exist for each type of problem. MATLAB provides built-in functions for these optimization problems and we will explore some of these functions. Since most of these functions follow a similar syntax, we will first learn a unified approach to understand how to use built-in optimization functions and then see some examples of a few of these functions.

Defining an Objective Function

First we need to define our objective function in the form of a MATLAB function. All optimization functions in MATLAB accept a function handle. This function can be primary or anonymous. Anonymous functions may be a better option when the objective is simple. Also, if the function is dependent on not only design parameters x but also some external inputs, e.g. constants c that are likely to be changed, it is better to create an anonymous function in the following way:

```
f=@(x) sin(x)-c/10;
```

This way we can solve multiple optimization problems for different values of c without defining more functions.

```
for c=1:10
f=@(x) sin(x)-c/10;
x(c+1)=fzero(f,[0 3.14]);
end
```

Defining Constraints

If the optimization has constraints over parameters, then we need to select a built-in function written specifically for constrained optimization and define the constraints to pass them to the selected function. There are various types of constraints and each can be defined in the following way:

Linear Constraints

Linear constraints can be of two types

1. Equalities of the form $A_{eq}(x) = B_{eq}$.
2. Inequalities of the form $A(x) \le B$.

Since both cases are linear constraints, they can be represented as matrices in the following way:

$$A_{eq}(x) = \mathbf{A_{eq}x}$$
$$A(x) = \mathbf{Ax}$$

We need to define these four matrices A_{eq}, A, B and B_{eq} to provide the constraints.

Nonlinear constraints

Similarly, nonlinear constraints can be of two types:

1. Equalities of the form $C_{eq}(x) = 0$.

2. Inequalities of the form $C(x) \leq 0$.

In both cases, as these are nonlinear constraints, they cannot be represented as matrices. So we have to define these constraints in the form of a function which takes x as input and returns C and C_{eq} as output for x. If one of the two constraints is missing, then the corresponding output matrix should be set to [ ].

Optimization Options

An optimization method has a few specifications to tweak the performance. We saw one such option in Chapter 6 while discussing tolerance for termination conditions. We can specify the display options (choosing whether a detailed step by step display is needed or only a final summary is required), the tolerance (such as x tolerance or function tolerance to determine the termination conditions), maximum evaluations or iterations (to avoid infinite iterations for non-solvable optimization problems).

To specify the options, we have to define a structure with attributes as fields and corresponding desired values and pass it as input to the built-in optimization function. If we want to change only a few of the options and leave other options as default, MATLAB's built-in optimset should be used to generate this option structure. The following lines of code

```
O=optimset('Display','iter','TolX','1e-6');
```

will set the two properties Display and TolX to be 'iter' and 1e-6 and leaves other properties at their default values. We can also specify an algorithm to force MATLAB to use that particular algorithm only. To view the whole set of options, we can use one of the following two commands

```
help optimset;
optimset(@fun)
```

where fun is the name of the built-in optimization function we want to use.

Problem Structures

Another way to specify all the parameters (such as function name, constraints, options) is to create a problem structure and directly pass this structure to the built-in optimization function as input.

Output Format

Most of the built-in functions will return the following values:

xopt: the optimal x where the function attains its optimal value (i.e. is minimal).
fminvalue: the function value at the optimal x xopt.

Exitflag: the integer flag used to denote whether the optimization was successful or terminated due to some problem. Positive exit flags correspond to successful outcomes. Negative exit flags correspond to unsuccessful outcomes where the solver has failed to compute an optimal solution. The zero exit flag corresponds to the solver being halted by exceeding an iteration limit or limit on the number of functions. The exact ids and interpretations for a specific function can be seen by typing help followed by the function name.

Output Structure: The output structure contains information about the optimization iterations and reason for termination. For example, an output structure may look like the following

```
output =
        iterations: 7
         funcCount: 8
      cgiterations: 7
     firstorderopt: 4.7948e-010
         algorithm: 'large-scale: trust-region Newton'
           message: [1x539 char]
```

Minimization Problems

In this subsection, we will see some of the widely used built-in functions provided by MATLAB for minimizing a function. Note that maximization can be achieved easily by performing a minimization over the negative or reciprocal of the function.

Unconstrained Minimization

Suppose we want to minimize $f(x)$ where x is a vector with no constraints over it. Here we can use fminunc (which stands for function **min**imization **unc**onstrained). Consider the function

$$f(x) = \cos(x+y) + x^2 + y^2$$

We can minimize this function using fminunc by following the unified approach we learned in the previous section.

```
f=@(x) cos(x(1)+x(2))+x(1)^2+x(2)^2;
x0=[0.1 0.1]; %initial guess
[x funcvalue]=fminunc(f,x0);
```

We can also use the primary functions to define the objective function. Consider the function $f(x) = e^{x_1}(7x_1^2 + 2x_2^2 + 2x_1x_2 - 2)$ which we need to minimize. First we define the objective function in a separate file func1.m

```
function y=func1(x)
x1=x(1);
x2=x(2);
y=exp(x1)*(7*x1*x1+2*x2*x2+2*x1*x2-2);
```

Then we can call fminunc in a separate script/function file

```
[x funx]=fminunc(@func1,[0 0]);
```

We can also use fminsearch, which uses the Nelder-Mead simplex (direct search) method and is a derivative-free method.

```
[x funcvalue]=fminsearch(fun,x0);
```

Scalar Minimization with Bounds

Suppose we are interested in solving $\min_x f(x)$ such that $l \leq x \leq u$, where x is a scalar. We can use the function fminbnd to solve such problems. Recall the example in the last section, the same problem can be solved using this built-in function.

```
lower_range=0;upper_range=1;
f=@(x) x^2+cos(4*x);
[x fminvalue]=fminbnd(f,lower_range,upper_range);
```

which gives as output the optimal x = 0.6964 and optimal function value fminvalue = -0.452.

Constrained Minimization

We can use the built-in function fmincon to solve optimization problems with constraints over the values of parameters. Consider the following problem:

$$\min_x f(x)$$

such that
$$l \leq x \leq u \quad ceq(x) = 0,$$
$$c(x) \leq 0,$$
$$Ax \leq B \quad Aeq\, x = Beq$$

The following code implements the constrained optimization problem: $\max_{x,y} xy$ such that $x + y = 5$

```
f=@(x) -x(1)*x(2);
Aeq=[1 1];Beq=5;
A=[];B=[];
XO=[1 4]';
X = fmincon(f,XO,A,B,Aeq,Beq);
```

Similarly the problem $\min_{x,y} x + y$ such that $xy = 4$ can be solved by the following code:

```
f=@(x) x(1)+x(2);
Aeq=[];Beq=[];A=[];B=[];
L=[];B=[];
XO=[1 4]';
X = fmincon(f,XO,A,B,Aeq,Beq,L,B,confunc_f);
```

where confunc_f is given as

```
[C Ceq]=confunc_f(x)
C=[];
Ceq=x(1)*x(2)-4;
```

Let us consider another constrained minimization with linear constraints. Suppose we need to minimize $f(x) = e^{x_1}(7x_1^2 + 2x_2^2 + 2x_1x_2 - 2)$ where $7x_1 + 2x_2 = 0$ and $2x_1 \leq 0$. Here we will first define the objective function using the primary function

```
function y=func2(x)
x1=x(1);
x2=x(2);
y=exp(x1)*(7*x1*x1+2*x2*x2+2*x1*x2-2);
```

Then we will define linear constraints using corresponding matrices in a separate script/function file

```
Ceq=[7 2];
Deq=0;
C=[2 0];
D=0;
```

and call fmincon in the same script/function file

```
[x]=fmincon(@func2,[0 .2],C,D,Ce,Deq);
```

Now suppose the constraints are $\sin(x_1) + \exp(x_2) \leq 2$. These constraints must be defined using a primary function in a separate function file

```
function [C Ceq]=funccon3(x)
x1=x(1);
x2=x(2);
C=sin(x1)+exp(x2)-2;
Ceq=[];
```

Then we can call fmincon in a separate script/function file

```
[x]=fmincon(@func2,[0 .2],[],[],[],[],[],[], funcon3);
```

Linear Programming

Consider the special case where the function $f(x)$ is a linear function of the form $\mathbf{f^T x}$. In such cases, we can also use the linprog function. The syntax of this function is as follows:

```
X = linprog(f,A,b,Aeq,beq,LB,UB,X0,OPTIONS);
X = linprog(f,A,b,Aeq,beq);
```

Quadratic Programming

Similarly, for functions of the form $\frac{1}{2}x^T H x + f^T x$, we can use the function quadprog which tends to give better results than those achieved using the general function fmincon.

```
X = quadprog(H,f,A,b,Aeq,beq,LB,UB);
```

Semi-infinite Minimization

Semi-infinite programs are of the following form
    $\min f(x)$ such that $K(x,w) \leq 0$ for $\forall w$,

$$c(x) \leq 0, \ c_{eq}(x) = 0,$$
$$Ax \leq b, \ A_{eq}x = b_{eq}, l \leq x \leq u$$

which can be solved using the seminf function whose syntax is given as

```
X = fseminf(f,x0,n_theta,seminf_function)
```

Here n_theta is the number of semi-infinite constraints and seminf_function is a function which accepts a value x and range S as input and returns the nonlinear equality and inequality constraints and n_theta semi-infinite constraints computed over x and the range S. Type help fseminf for more information.

Multi-objective Problems

Sometimes, we need to maximize a multivariate function with respect to some variables and minimize it with respect to other variables. Consider a function $f:R^d \to R^n$ which takes a vector x as input and returns an n dimensional vector. Let us denote the ith element by the function $f:R^d \to R$. Now the optimization problem $\min_i \max_x f_i(x)$ such that $l \leq x \leq u$, $c(x) = 0$, $c_{eq}(x) = 0$, $Ax \leq b$, $A_{eq}x = b_{eq}$ can be solved using the built-in MATLAB function fminimax. The syntax of the function with a simple example is given in the following code

```
fun=@(x) [x.^2+0.1; x.^4; x+cos(x)];
x = fminimax(fun,x0,A,b,Aeq,beq,lb,ub,nonlcon,options);
```

Equation Solving

Solving any equation can also be represented as an optimization problem. For example, suppose we want to compute the solution of the equation $f(x) = 0$. Note that the minimum $f(x)^2$ can achieve is 0. So the optimization problem $\min_x f(x)^2$ will also give us the same result.

Linear Equations

Consider the linear equation $Ax = b$ which is widely used in many engineering applications. If the inverse of A exists, the solution is given as $x = A^{-1}b$. In the cases where the inverse of A doesn't exist or if the equations are not consistent, we try to find a closest solution x. In other words, we try to find an x that minimizes the error $|(|Ax-b|)|^2$, which is called the least-squares optimization. Note that this will give same solution as $A^{-1}b$ when the latter is possible. To solve this optimization, we can use MATLAB's blackslash operator

```
X=A\b;
```

Nonlinear Equations of One Variable

We have seen that the function fzero computes the zero of a nonlinear function $f(x)$ of one variable. This is equivalent to solving the equation $f(x)=0$.

```
x = fzero(@func1,x0);
```

Nonlinear Equations of Several Variables

Similarly fsolve can be used to solve a multivariable equation of the form $F(\mathbf{x})=0$. The syntax is similar to fzero, however here x is a vector.

```
x = fsolve(@func1,x0)
```

Summary

In this chapter, we have learnt the concept of optimization. We first learnt how to implement an optimization method to minimize a function. We then learnt about the MATLAB Optimization Toolbox, which provides us with many built-in functions for various kinds of optimization problems. Since we cannot talk about all of them in detail, we first described a unified approach to all these functions which includes their common syntax, input and output structures. Then we discussed a few widely used functions with examples.

CHAPTER 8

■ ■ ■

Evolutionary Computations

In Chapter 7, we discussed many optimization algorithms and inbuilt MATLAB functions, and we saw examples of their use. However, almost all of these algorithms are gradient-based and return only local minima. If the objective function has many local minima and we start from an initial guess close to one such minimum, the algorithm will most probably output the local minimum closest to the initial guess. In such cases, we would never reach the global minimum. Hence the success of the method depends highly on the initial guess. Most real world objectives are multivariate functions and contain multiple minima. Therefore, new heuristic search-based algorithms have been devised. These algorithms start with multiple initial guesses and result in solutions which evolve with time. Hence these methods are known as evolutionary computation methods.

Every initial guess initiates its own optimization chain containing values updated at each step. At any step, the value from a chain is known as a candidate solution. The set of all candidate solutions from a single step is known as a population. Since the updates are performed at every step for all the chains, we need to use simple and less extensive computations at each step rather than performing steps involving gradients or Hessians. In this chapter, we will study two algorithms of this kind and learn how we can implement them. These algorithms are inspired by nature and natural processes, motivated by the belief that nature is the best optimizer.

The Rastrigin Function

In this chapter, we will consider a special benchmark function, known as the Rastrigin function, which is used to evaluate the performance of optimization methods. It is a non-convex function with multiple local minima and one global minimum. This is a perfect example which illustrates why a gradient-based optimization algorithm will not always work. The Rastrigin function in two dimensions is given by

$$f(x_1, x_2) = 20 + x_1^2 - 10\cos 2\pi x_1 + x_2^2 - 10\cos 2\pi x_2$$

which is plotted in Figure 8-1 for $x \in [-1.2, 1.2]$. As is clear from the figure, this function has multiple minima and one global minimum. In the next two sections, we will discuss two evolutionary computation algorithms, namely PSO and GA, which are able to solve these kinds of difficult optimization problems. Before moving forward, let us first define this function in MATLAB in the following way

```
function f=rastrigin(x)
s=x.^2-10*cos(2*pi*x);
f=20+sum(s);
```

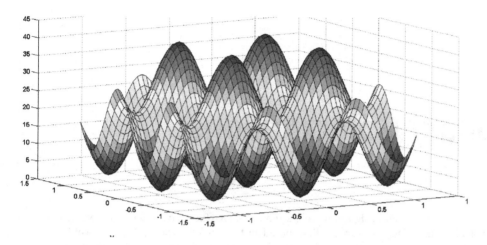

Figure 8-1. *The Rastrigin function*

The above implementation of the function accepts a vector x representing a candidate solution and computes the value of the Rastrigin function, treating each element of the vector as one dimension/variable. Let us define a vectorized version of the Rastrigin function which accepts a matrix Xpop representing the whole population. Here each row of Xpop is a candidate solution. The following MATLAB function implements the same.

```
function f=rastrigin_vec(Xpop)
s=Xpop.^2-10*cos(2*pi*Xpop);
f=20+sum(s,2);
```

Here the output f is a vector with each element representing the function value at the corresponding candidate solution.

Particle Swarm Optimization

Particle swarm optimization (PSO) is an optimization algorithm from the class of evolutionary computation methods and is inspired by the procedure by which a swarm of birds finds its food or optimum habitat.

In PSO, the population is known as a swarm and each candidate solution is called a particle. The objective is to minimize a function $f(\mathbf{x})$ where x denotes a particle. We start with an initial population. For any particle, a position $\mathbf{x}$ is said to be better than a position $\mathbf{y}$ if $f(\mathbf{x}) < f(\mathbf{y})$ Now the population is updated by the movement of particles around the search space. Each particle i remembers the best position P_i attained by it in the past. Also the swarm remembers the global best value G attained by any particle in the past. Each particle's movement is determined by its current velocity, its own best known position and the global best value of the swarm. The swarm is expected to move towards the global best solution or at least towards a satisfactory solution for which the function value is close to the global minimum.

Algorithm

The algorithm is given as follows:)

Initialization

1. Define N=size of population.

2. Generate N particles randomly in the search space.

3. Denote the location of the ith particle by x_i.

4. Randomly generate the velocity v_i of the particles.

5. Define the velocity weight factor $w = 0.5$.

6. For each particle, set $P_i=x_i$.

7. Compute the value f_i as $f_i=f(x_i)$ for each particle.

8. Find the particle that has the minimum f_i among all particles. Set G to it.

Iterations and Updates

9. Now for each particle i

    a. Generate two uniform random variables r_1 and r_2.

    b. Compute $v_{(i,next)}=wv_i+C_1r_1(P_i\text{-}x_i)+C_2r_2(G\text{-}x_i)$.

    c. Compute $x_{(i,next)} =x_i+v_i$.

    d. If $f(x_{i,next})<f(x_i)$

    i. Update $Pi=xi,next$.

    e. Update the velocity vi of the particle by $v_{i,next}$.

    f. Update the location of the particle by $x_i next$.

10. Compute the minimum of all $f(P_i)$ and set the corresponding particle to G.

11. If the terminate conditions are met, go to step 11, otherwise go to step 8.

Output

12. Output G as the solution of the optimization.

Here C_1 and C_2 are two parameters which define the weighting assigned to the guidance given by the local best value and the global best value.

Implementation

In this section, we will see how we can implement PSO as a generic function. Our goal is to create a function which accepts a handle to the objective function and a few configuration parameters as inputs, performs the steps of the PSO algorithm and outputs the optimal solution. Let us first implement it as a script and assume that the following three variables are given to us)

```
objfunction %handle to function
nvars %number of independent variables
opt %structure with following configuration fields
%opt.C1     % Cognitive parameter
%opt.C2     % Social parameter
%opt.N      % Size of swarm
%opt.UB     % Upper limit of search space, must be a 1xnvars vector
%opt.LB     % Lower limit of search space, must be a 1xnvars vector
%opt.MaxIter %maximum number of iterations
%opt.MinIter % minimum number of iteration to terminate when
                          % global best is not changing much
%opt.TolG  % tolerance to compare the change in global best
```

Now we will implement each part of the algorithm.

Initialization

```
N=opt.N;
X= repmat(opt.LB,N,1)+repmat(opt.UB-Out.LB,N,1).*rand(N,nvars);
Vrange=2*opt.UB;
V=-repmat(Vrange,N,1)+2*repmat(Vrange,N,1).*rand(N,nvars);
f=objfunction(X);
P=X; %initialize pbest with the initial particles locations
[Gbestval G]=min(f);
termination=0; %termination flag to decide when to terminate
iter=1;
```

Note that we initialized each particle's velocity by creating a vector with uniform random variables between 0 and 1 and then scaled it so that it falls inside the range [2opt.LB, 2opt.UB].

Iteration Loop

```
while (termination ==0)
```

Updates

```
C1=opt.C1;C2=opt.C2;
                for i=1:N
                        %compute next step velocities and locations
                        vnext=0.5*V(i,:)+...
                                C1*rand(1,2).*(P(i,:)-X(i,:))...
                                +C2*rand(1,2).* (G-X(i,:));
                        xnext=X(i,:)+vnext;
                        %update the pbest if the next computed values are
                        %better than the current values
                        if objfunction(xnext)<objfunction(P(i,:)
                                P(i,:)=xnext;
                        end
                        V(i,:)=vnext;
                        X(i,:)=xnext;
                end
                f=objfunction(P);
                %compute the global best particle
                [Gbestval indexG]=min(f);
                G=P(indexG,:);
                Sol(iter,:)=G;
                iter=iter+1;
```

Termination Conditions

```
if iter>opt.MaxIter
        termination=1;
end
if iter>opt.MinIter+1
        %check if the value of G hasn't changed from past
        %MinIter number of iterations.
        e=abs(Sol(iter-1,:)-Sol(iter-opt.MinIter-1,:));
        if e<opt.TolG
                termination=1;
        end
end
```

Iteration Ends and Outputs

```
end
optSol=Sol(end,:);
optValue=objfunction(optSol);
optTrace =Sol;
```

Function Definition

Now we will transform the script into a primary function by adding the following line at the start of the script file.

```
function [optSol optValue optTrace]=solvePSO(objfunction,nvars,opt);
```

Example

Now we can define the objective function that we want to optimize along with configuration parameters in a separate script/function file and call the solvePSO in the following way:

```
objfunction =@rastrigin_vec;
nvars =2;
opt.C1    = 2;
opt.C2    = 2;
opt.N     = 30;
opt.UB    = [1.2 1.2];
opt.LB    = [-1.2 -1.2];
opt.MaxIter =60;
opt.MinIter =30;
opt.TolG  = 1e-5;
[optS optV trace]=solvePSO(objfunction,nvars,opt);
```

Then the following code can plot the objective function value at the global best particle at each step (see Figure 8-2)

```
plot(1:size(trace,1),objfunction(trace),'LineWidth',2);
```

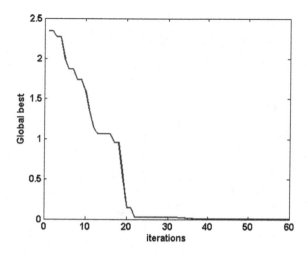

Figure 8-2. *Convergence of the PSO algorithm for the Rastrigin function*

We can also plot the movement of the global best particle with respect to iteration time (see Figure 8-3) in the following way:

```
plot(trace(:,1),trace(:,2),'LineWidth',2);
```

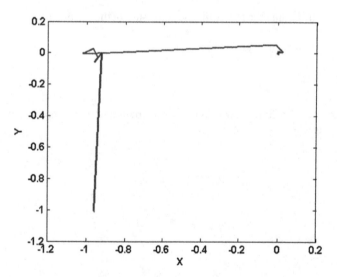

Figure 8-3. *Trace path of global best in a sample execution of PSO for the Rastrigin function*

The Genetic Algorithm

The genetic algorithm (GA) is a particular example of an evolutionary algorithm (EA) that uses techniques inspired by evolutionary biology such as inheritance, mutation, selection, and crossover (also called recombination). It imitates the natural reproduction and selection process where genes combine to generate a better offspring. We will discuss different steps of the genetic algorithm and the way to implement each step. In GA, the objective function is also called the fitness function as it determines the capability of any candidate solution to survive and reproduce.

Representation

In a natural evolution process, there are multiple chromosomes (each representing one individual) at any generation and they make up the population. In GA, we also have multiple candidate solutions at any step (a step is also known as a generation) which make up the solution population. Each candidate solution imitates a single chromosome or genotype (hence represents an individual) and is represented by a binary vector where each binary value represents a gene (see Figure 8-4). We will fix the length of the vector to simplify the key operations. For example, if there are five candidate solution values (x= 5,6,7,2,10) in any population, we can represent the population by the following matrix

```
Xpop=   [0 0 0 0 0 1 0 1;  ...
         0 0 0 0 0 1 1 0;  ...
                 0 0 0 0 0 1 1 1;  ...
                 0 0 0 0 0 0 1 0; ...
                 0 0 0 1 0 1 0];
```

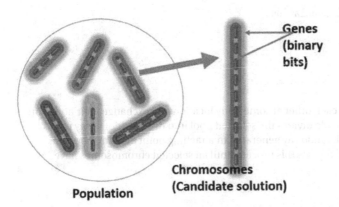

Figure 8-4. Representation of a candidate solution by a chromosome in a genetic algorithm

If there is more than one variable, we can append the binary representation of all the variables to make a big vector. For example, if there are three candidate solutions (x= (1,5),(6,10),(7,2)) in any population, we can represent the population as

```
Xpop=   [0 0 0 0 0 0 0 1 0 0 0 0 0 1 0 1;  ...
         0 0 0 0 0 1 1 0 0 0 0 0 1 0 1 0;  ...
         0 0 0 0 0 1 1 1 0 0 0 0 0 0 1 0];
```

Initialization

Let N denote the population size, nvars denote the number of variables and nbits denote the number of bits needed to represent each variable. We can see that each chromosome can be represented by nvars*nbits bits. To initialize the population, we will first generate nvars*nbits random values from a uniform distribution for each chromosome and then convert each of these random values to a binary value.

```
N=opt.N;
nbits=opt.nbits;
XInitPop=rand(N,nvars*nbits)<0.5;
XPop     = XInitPop;
```

Selection

At each generation, some candidates are selected for reproduction. This selection is made according to their fitness value. In this implementation, we would select the top 50% of the population to reproduce. Let fitnessfunction be the handle of the fitness function.

```
f=fitnessfunction(XPop);
selectionratio =0.5;

%sort the chromosomes in terms of their fitness values
[fsort indexsort]=sort(f,1,'descend');
XPop=XPop(indexsort,:);

%select the top selectionratio % of the total population
indexselect= 1:floor(N*selectionratio);
nselect = length(indexselect);
```

Crossover

In crossover operations, two chromosomes attach to each other at some body location and exchange their body with each other as illustrated in Figure 8-5. The following code divides the selected pool into two partitions (say males and females), takes one chromosome from each pool, randomly generates an attaching point in them, performs the crossover to generate two new chromosomes and repeats this process until all selected chromosomes have participated in reproduction.

```
%shuffle the order of selected chromosomes
Indexselect      =indexselect(randperm(nselect));

%divide into two pools
indexmales       =indexselect(1:floor(nselect/2));
indexfemales     =indexselect(1+floor(nselect/2):end);
nchildren= floor(nselect/2)*2;
for i=1:length(indexmales)
        father= XPop(indexmales(i),:);
        mother= XPop(indexfemales(i),:);
        %find random attaching bit position
        attachbit=1+floor(rand(1,1)*nbits);
        %perform crossover
```

```
        child1= [father(1:attachbit-1) mother(attachbit:end)];
        child2= [mother(1:attachbit-1) father(attachbit:end)];

        children(i*2-1,:)         = child1;
        children(i*2,:) = child2;
end
```

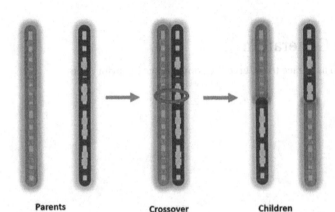

Parents   **Crossover**   **Children**

Figure 8-5. *Illustration of a crossover function in a chromosome in a genetic alogrithm*

Note to generate the random bit position for attachment, we first generate a random uniform variable between 0 and 1. We then scale it so that it falls between 0 and nbits. Then we take the floor of this number which will result in a random integer uniformly distributed between 0 and nbits. We finally add 1 so that it becomes a random integer uniformly distributed between 1 and nbits.

Mutation

In the mutation operation, a randomly picked gene of a randomly picked chromosome gets inverted, leading to a child which may have very different properties than the parent. The following code takes 10% of the selected population (which is 5% of the complete population), selects a random bit position at each selected chromosome and flips the bit to generate a new child.

```
%find random 10% of the mutants from the selected population
indexmutants=indexselect(randperm(length(indexselect)));
nmutants=floor(nselect*0.1);
indexmutants=indexmutants(1:nmutants);

%generate the nmutants number of mutation bit locations, one for %each mutant parent chromosome
mutationbits=1+floor(rand(nmutants,1)*nbits);

%select the mutant values
valuemutants = XPop(indexmutants,: );

%flip the bit
valuemutants(:,mutationbits)=1-valuemutants(:,mutationbits);
mutantchildren=valuemutants;
```

New Generation

Finally we let the bottom 55% (50+5) of the population die and fill it with children to create the next generation.

```
XPopNew=XPop;
XPopNew(end-nmutants+1:end,:)=mutantchildren;
XPopNew(end-nmutants+1-nchildren:end-nmutants,:)=children;
XPop=XPopNew;
```

Store the Best Chromosome of the Generation

We will store the best chromosome at each generation as a trace to observe the convergence behavior of our implementation.

```
f=fitnessfunction(XPop);
[fbest indexbestchromosome]=max(f);
optTrace(iter,:)=XPop(indexbestchromosome,:);
```

Termination Conditions

```
iter=iter+1;
if iter>opt.MaxIter
        termination=1;
end
```

Iterations

The above discussed steps involving selection, crossover, mutation and formation of a new generation must be repeated using a while loop until the termination condition is met.

```
iter=1;
while(termination==0)
        % code follows here

end
```

Output

```
optSol=optTrace(end,:);
[optV optSolReal]=fitnessfunction(optSol);
```

Note that for the last line of the above code, the fitness function must adhere to a syntax. See the example section to learn the exact syntax required to run this implementation.

Function Definition

Let us convert the above written code into a function by adding the following lines at the beginning of the file.

```
function [optSol optSolReal optV optTrace] =solveGA(fitnessfunction,nvars,opt)
```

Example

We will now apply our solveGA function to solve the Rastrigin optimization problem. Let us first define an intermediate interface function which can process the chromosome representation of the population and generate the fitness of each candidate solution from the rastrigin_vec function.

First we need to define how the binary representation is linked to the actual value. Suppose the range of the variable is $[a,b]$ and the number of bits assigned to each variable is nbits. Note that a binary string with nbits will represent a value between 0 to $2^{nbits}-1$ which can be scaled to a value between 0 to 1 by dividing the original value by $2^{nbits}-1$. Finally, we can scale the result again to transform it to the corresponding value between a and b.

```
function [f y]=fitness_interface(XPop,nvars,nbits,range)
a=range(1);
b=range(2);
for i=1:size(XPop,1)
        x=XPop(i,:);
        for j=1:nvars
                bitrange= (j-1)*nbits+(1:nbits)
                y(i,j)=bin2dec(num2str(x(bitrange)));
        end
end
y=a+(b-a)*y/(2^nbits-1);
f=-rastrigin_vec(y);
```

Notice the negative sign. It is there because GA maximizes the fitnessfunction whereas our goal here is to minimize the Rastrigin function.

The following code defines the final fitness function that can be passed to solveGA along with configuration parameters and calls the solveGA:

```
nvars=2;
nbits=10;
range=[-1.2 1.2];
fitnessfunction=@(x) fitness_interface(XPop,nvars,nbits,range);
opt.MaxIter=70;
opt.N=50;
opt.nbits=nbits;
[optSol ptSolReal optVal optTraceoptTrace]= ...
                                solveGA(fitnessfunction,nvars,opt);
```

We can plot the optimum best fitness value achieved at each generation (see Figure 8-6) using the following code:

```
[optTraceValue optTraceReal]=fitnessfunction(optTrace);
plot(optTraceReal(:,1),optTraceReal(:,2),'-','LineWidth',2);
```

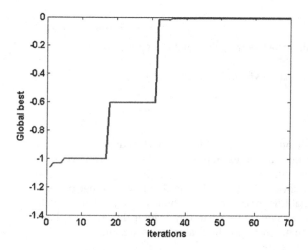

Figure 8-6. *Convergence of the genetic algorithm for the Rastrigin function*

The Inbuilt Function ga

MATLAB provides an inbuilt method ga to solve any optimization problem using the genetic algorithm. Note that you need to have the Genetic Algorithm Toolbox installed to use this inbuilt function. Like other inbuilt optimization functions, we need to first define the objective function or the fitness function. For the example we considered, we can implement the fitness function in the following way

```
function f=fitness_rastrigin(x)
s=x.^2-10*cos(2*pi*x);
f=20+sum(s);
```

Note that the inbuilt function ga will try to minimize the fitness function. This is opposite to the previous convention used in our GA implementation, where we wanted to maximize the fitness function.

We can also implement the function in the vectorized fashion so that it accepts the complete population XPop as input where each row in XPop represents a single candidate solution. This can help ga to run faster, which will be investigated later.

Now in a separate function/scriptfile, we define nvars by the total number of parameters, which is 2 here. To use the genetic algorithm at the command line, we can now call the genetic algorithm function ga with the following syntax

```
nvars=2;
[xopt fval] = ga(@fitness, nvars)
```

The function ga will return the following outputs
xopt   Optimal point at which the final value is attained
fval   Value of the fitness function at xopt

Simulation options

The genetic algorithm has many configuration parameters and its performance can be fine-tuned by adjusting parameters. The function ga also accepts an extra input options in the following syntax.

```
[x fval] = ga(@fitnessfun, nvars, options)
```

Here options is a structure containing various simulation parameters and configuration settings for the genetic algorithm. If we do not pass this argument, ga uses the default options. To create the options structure, we should use the inbuilt function gaoptimset. With its help, we need to pass only the options which we want to change and the rest of the options which are not passed are automatically set to their default values. The structure of the variable options is given below.

```
options =
           PopulationType: 'doubleVector'
            PopInitRange: [2x1 double]
           PopulationSize: 20
              EliteCount: 2
        CrossoverFraction: 0.8000
          ParetoFraction: []
       MigrationDirection: 'forward'
        MigrationInterval: 20
        MigrationFraction: 0.2000
              Generations: 100
               TimeLimit: Inf
             FitnessLimit: -Inf
            StallGenLimit: 50
           StallTimeLimit: Inf
                   TolFun: 1.0000e-006
                   TolCon: 1.0000e-006
       InitialPopulation: []
           InitialScores: []
           InitialPenalty: 10
            PenaltyFactor: 100
             PlotInterval: 1
              CreationFcn: @gacreationuniform
       FitnessScalingFcn: @fitscalingrank
             SelectionFcn: @selectionstochunif
            CrossoverFcn: @crossoverscattered
              MutationFcn: {[1x1 function_handle]  [1]  [1]}
       DistanceMeasureFcn: []
               HybridFcn: []
                  Display: 'final'
                 PlotFcns: []
               OutputFcns: []
               Vectorized: 'off'
              UseParallel: 'never'
```

Consider an example where we want to increase the population size to 200 and leave the other options unchanged. The following code will generate the desired options structure

```
Op=gaoptimset('PopulationSize',200);
```

and then we can call the ga function with the above options structure

```
X=ga(@fitness,2,Op);
```

We can see a configuration parameter 'Vectorized' which is set to off by default. This means that MATLAB expects a fitness function that is not vectorized and therefore ga will call fitnessfunction once for each candidate solution. Instead, we can change the fitness function in the following way so that the complete population can be passed at once to the fitnessfunction and it should be able to evaluate the fitness for all candidate solutions from that population.

```
function f=fitness_rastrigin_vec(Xpop)
s=Xpop.^2-10*cos(2*pi*Xpop);
f=20+sum(s,2);
```

Then we should let GA know that fitnessfunction is now vectorized by setting the 'Vectorized' option to on in the options structure and passing this options structure to ga

```
Op=gaoptimset('Vectorized','on');
X=ga(@fitnessvec,2,Op);
```

GUI Interface

MATLAB provides a graphical user interface to solve various kinds of optimization problems. This is helpful to those researchers who don't want to write a program and are more comfortable working with GUI-based software. To open the GA graphical user interface, type the following in the command window

```
optimtool('ga');
```

This will open a GA GUI. Now in the GUI, we can set different options and constraints. Once we are done, we can run the genetic algorithm method by clicking the run button. We can also see real time plots of convergence as the algorithm advances.

Summary

Evolutionary computation methods are meta-heuristic methods that help us to solve complex problems. They are able to learn the optimal pattern during execution. Two important classes of evolutionary computation methods are swarm intelligence and evolutionary algorithms. In this chapter, we have learnt two such algorithms, one from each class. The first algorithm, PSO, is a swarm intelligence algorithm and mimics the way birds find their food. The second algorithm, GA, is an evolutionary algorithm which mimics the process of natural evolution to generate the best species. We implemented both algorithms from scratch. As a side product, this chapter has also taught us in great detail how we can implement a complex algorithm.

CHAPTER 9

■ ■ ■

Regression and Model Fitting

In previous chapters, we have discussed methods for simulating a system defined by a particular model, but we haven't talked about how to build such a model or verify that the model we are using is correct or suitable. Building/finding the optimal model for any system is one of the most important tasks in any engineering design. If the system is simple, we can study the physics behind it and come up with an analytical and mathematical model. But most real world systems are very complex and finding an exact model for them is very difficult. Another way to build a model is by empirical fitting. In this method, we first perform a series of experiments on the system to collect samples of input and output signals. Then we try to find a relation between output and inputs with some basic assumptions about the system. Given any two data sets, the derivation of a relation is known as regression. In this chapter, we will first learn the basic concepts and methods of regression and then use this knowledge to perform model fitting.

Regression

Regression is a general term for any method which computes the relation between two or more data variables using many samples of these variables. In practice, we assume some generic relation model, e.g. we can assume the relationship is linear (linear regression) or a polynomial of order m (nonlinear regression). Since the data samples are acquired using some experiments, we have to consider the possibility of errors. There are different models for incorporating errors of which the Gaussian random error model is the most commonly used.

Linear Regression

Let us describe a very simple example of linear regression between two variables x & y. Let datax and datay denote the n samples of x and y respectively, collected via some experiment. We assume the following linear relation between x and y

$$y = ax + b$$

where the a and b are the parameters of the model and need to be determined by regression. Since the data collection is prone to error, we consider the following random error linear model instead

$$y_i = ax_i + b + e_i$$

where x_i & y_i denotes the ith data sample for x and y respectively and the error $e_i \sim N(0, s^2)$. The idea is to choose a and b so that they minimize the error variance or equivalently, the mean square error of the model given by

$$e_{mse} = \sqrt{\frac{1}{N} \sum_i (y_i - ax_i - b)^2}.$$

There are multiple ways to solve this problem:

Polynomial Fitting

We can regard this problem as a fitting of a first order polynomial to the data pair (x,y). Using the polyfit function (see Chapter 3 for details), we can easily estimate the value of a and b.

```
p=polyfit(datax,datay,1);
a=p(1);
b=p(2);
```

We get p=[0.0995 0.4004]. To validate the results of the regression, we can compute the mean square error between the simulated data from the fitted model and the actual data in the following way:

```
simdatay=a*datax+b;
err=sqrt(mean((datay-simdatay).^2));
```

which gives the error err =0.029. We can also visualize the goodness of fit via a scatter plot using the following code (see Figure 9-1)

```
scatter(datax,datay,'r')
hold on;
xr=0:10;
plot(xr,a*xr+b,'Linewidth',2)
createfigure(' ',' ');
```

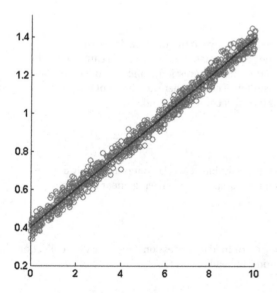

Figure 9-1. *Fitted linear model using linear regression*

The goodness of the fit can be evaluated quantitatively using the coefficient of determination (R-squared) given by

$$R_{sq} = 1 - \frac{SS_{res}}{SS_{tot}} = 1 - \frac{\sum (y_i - f(y_i))^2}{\sum (y_i - \sum y_i)^2}$$

which represents the percentage of variance that the selected model can explain. It can be computed by the following code

```
n=length(datay);
SSresid = err*n;
SStotal = (n-1) * var(y);
rsq = 1 - SSresid/SStotal;
```

Note that we have generated some dummy data to test our method (before trying it on actual experimental data) via the following piece of code:

```
datax=10*rand(1000,1);
datay=0.1*datax+0.4+0.03*randn(size(datax));
```

Optimization

Since a regression problem tries to minimize the mean square error, we can consider it as the following optimization problem:

$$S_L : \left\{ a_{opt}, b_{opt} \right\} = \underset{a,b}{\operatorname{argmin}} \frac{1}{N} \sum_i (y_i - ax_i - b)^2 = \underset{a,b}{\operatorname{argmin}} \sum_i (y_i - ax_i - b)^2$$

which can be solved by either of the following two methods:

1. By solving a general optimization problem in the following way:

    ```
    f=@(A) mean((datay-A(1)*datax-A(2)).^2);
    [A fminval]=fminunc(f,[1;1]);
    a=A(1);b=A(2);
    ```

2. By solving a linear equation:

    Consider a dummy variable $z_i = 1 \ \forall \ i$. So the optimization problem S_L can be written as

    $$\underset{a,b}{\operatorname{argmin}} \sum_i (y_i - ax_i - bz_i)^2.$$

If we let $A = \begin{bmatrix} x_1 & z_1 \\ x_2 & z_2 \\ x_3 & z_3 \\ \ldots \\ x_n & z_n \end{bmatrix}, X = \begin{bmatrix} a \\ b \end{bmatrix}$ & $Y = \begin{bmatrix} y_1 \\ y_2 \\ \ldots \\ y_n \end{bmatrix}$, we can see that the above optimization is equivalent to solving

the problem $\min_A \|AX\text{-}Y\|^2$. The solution to the latter problem is simply $X_{opt} = A^+B$ (A^+ denotes the pseudo-inverse of A) which can be computed in the following way:

```
%Dummy variable for intercept
dataz=ones(size(datax));
A= [datax dataz]\datay;
a=A(1);
b=A(2);
```

Nonlinear Regression

Nonlinear regression involves estimation of parameters for a nonlinear relationship among data variables and can be performed using similar procedures as linear regression. A nonlinear model can either be a polynomial function or a transcendental function. Let us consider both types of nonlinear regression one by one:

Polynomial Fitting

If the relationship between data variables x and y can be modelled by a polynomial of degree m given by

$$y_i = \sum_{j=1:m} a_j x_i^j + b,$$

where a_j, b are the coefficients of the polynomial (and hence parameters of the model), we can use the polyfit function to compute a_j, b in the following way

```
m=3;
p=polyfit(datax,datay,m);
a=p(1:end-1);b=p(end);
```

For nonlinear regressions, goodness of fit is measured by adjusted Rsquare, which can be computed by the following code

```
n=length(datay);
simy=sum(repmat(a,n,1)...
        .*(repmat(datax,1,m).^(repmat(m:-1:1,n,1))),2)+b;
err=sqrt(mean((datay-simy).^2));

SSresid = err*n;
SStotal = (n-1) * var(datay);
rsqadjusted = 1 - (n-1)/(n-1-m)*SSresid/SStotal;
```

General nonlinear Fitting

On the other hand, if the relationship is a non-polynomial relation, we need to use the optimization method to find the parameters of the model. The optimization criterion is to minimize the mean square error between the fitted value and the actual data values. Consider the following optimization problem:

Given a data pair [datax = $\{x_i\}$, datay = y_i] and a model $y = f(A,x)$ dependent on some parameters A, choose A such that $f(A,x)$ fits y in the least-squares sense, i.e. A solves the following optimization problem

$$A_{opt} = \underset{A}{\operatorname{argmin}} \sum_i \left\| f\left(A, x_i\right) - y_i \right\|^2.$$

A_{opt} is the optimal solution of the above minimization problem. Also, we can say that A_{opt} is the estimated parameters or fitted value of the parameters or $y = f(A_{opt}, x)$ is the fitted value model and is known as the predicted or simulated value of y at any x_i.

Let us take an example where the suggested model is $y = a \cos(\omega x) + b \sin(\omega x)$, which is dependent on three parameters a, b & ω whose values have to be determined by the regression. We can easily estimate the parameters in the following way:

```
f=@(A) sum((y-A(1)*cos(A(3)*x)-A(2)*sin(A(3)*x)).^2);
[Aopt]=fminunc(f,[.1 .2 19.5]');
```

Here f denotes the handle of an anonymous function which computes the mean square error for any values of parameters for given x and y. Note that instead of defining the one line anonymous function for fixed x and y, we can also define a general model function as

```
function e=func3(A,x,y)
a=A(1);
b=A(2);
omega=A(3);
y1=a*cos(omega*x)+b*cos(omega*x);
e=sum((y-y1).^2);
```

and then create an anonymous function specifically for the given data by the following code

```
f=@(A) func3(A,x,y);
```

Note that we can generate some dummy data to test our method (before trying it on actual experimental data) by the following piece of code:

```
x=0:.001:10;
y=.2*cos(20*x)+.3*sin(20*x)+.02*rand(size(x));
```

The Inbuilt Function Nlinfit

We can also use the nlinfit function provided by the MATLAB Statistics Toolbox to fit any nonlinear model. The syntax of nlinfit is the following:

```
betafit = nlinfit(X,Y,modelfun,beta0)
```

where X is the independent data, Y is the dependent data, modelfun is the function representing the model $y = f(\beta, x)$ with parameter β, and beta0 is the initial guess for the parameter β. betafit is the estimated value of the parameter β returned by nlinfit.

111

The model function modefun should have the following definition format:

```
function y= modelfun(beta,x)
```

This function should accept as parameters a vector β and a value of x and should return the predicted value of y for the model $y=f(\beta,x)$ at x.

Let us consider the previous example. Our model function should look like

```
function y=func_model(A,x)
a=A(1);
b=A(2);
omega=A(3);
y=a*cos(omega*x)+b*sin(omega*x);
```

Now in a separate file, we can define the data and call the nlinfit function in the following way

```
Azero=[0.1 0.2 19.8]';
Afit = nlinfit(x,y,@func_model,Azero)
```

which will return estimated values of the model parameters.

Generalized Linear Regression

A generalized linear model (GLM) is a generalization of linear regression. In this model, the response variable is modeled as a general function (known as an inverse link) of the linear combination of independent variables (covariates) with an error term from any arbitrary distribution. In other words, the response variable y_i is modeled as

$$y_i \sim F(\mu_i),$$

$$\mu_i = g^{-1}\left(\sum_j a_j x_{ij}\right).$$

Here $g(\cdot)$ is the link function, $F(\cdot)$ is some probability distribution, $\{x_{ij}; j \in [1:m]\}$ are the covariates and y_i is the response variable for the ith data sample. The distribution function F and link function g together define the class of GLM. For example, one class of GLM model is the Poisson Log GLM which has a Poisson distributed response variable and log link function. The linear regression is a special case of GLM with Gaussian distribution and identity link function.

The MATLAB Statistics Toolbox has the inbuilt glmfit function which can be used to perform a GLM regression. You need to specify both the distribution function and the link function.

Consider an example where we performed a set of six experiments to study the effect of a particular drug on rats. The ith experiment consists of n_i rats. Let y_i be the number of rats that died at the end of the ith experiment. Let x_i denote the amount of drugs given to the rats and z_i denote the amount of daily food given to each rat in the ith experiment. The following data was documented at the end of the experiment.

```
n=[10 10 10 10 10 10]';
x=[10 4 .5 9 12 5]';
y=[20  15  1 5 10  13]';
z=[300 200 330 250 270 473]';
```

Let us fit a GLM with binomial distribution and logit function. The GLM for a binomial response variable requires the following inputs:

X: covariates matrix, each column representing one covariate

Y: [y n] two column matrix with the first column containing the response variable and the second containing values of n.

The following code calls glmfit and displays the regression results

```
g = fitglm(x,[y n],'linear','distr','binomial','link','probit')
```

The interested readers are referred to the MATLAB documentation on glmfit for more on how to call glmfit for various classes of GLM models from the following link http://www.mathworks.com/help/stats/generalized-linear-regression.html.

Time Series Analysis

A time series is a sequence of data points of a single variable at uniform time intervals. For example, a time series can be created by collecting the price of a particular stock at 10am every day for a month. In time series analysis, we are interested in studying the relationship between the current value and previous values of the variable. Information about this dependence can help us in predicting the future values of the variable based on current values. The basic idea behind time series analysis is to create multiple but delayed copies of the same data. Let us consider an example of rainfall in a particular city where the data is collected every day for a month. Let $x[i]$ denote the amount of rainfall in day i. To create the delayed data, we create copies of the same data in the following way

```
xprev2=x(1:end-2);
xprev1=x(2:end-1);
xcurrent=x(3:end);
```

Here xcurrent denotes the current data (xcurrent[i] denotes the data of day $i+2$), xprev1 denotes the previous day's data (day $i+1$) and xprev2 denotes the data of the day before yesterday.

Autocorrelation and Proposing Models

To analyze the dependency on the previous values, let us first analyze the autocorrelation of the given data

```
for i=0:10
        xc=x(i+1:end);
        xdelayedbyi=x(1:end-i);
        t=corrcoef(xc,xdelayedbyi);
        xcorr1(i+1)=t(1,2);
end
plot(0:10,xcorr1);
```

which is plotted in Figure 9-2. The autocorrelation shows that the current data is highly dependent on yesterday's data and the data from two days before. Therefore, we propose a relation

$$x[n] = ax[n-1] + bx[n-3]$$

to model the given data. Here $z_1 = y[n-1]$ and $z_2 = x[n-3]$ are the covariates and $y[n] = x[n]$ is the response variable. Such a model is known as an autoregressive model.

113

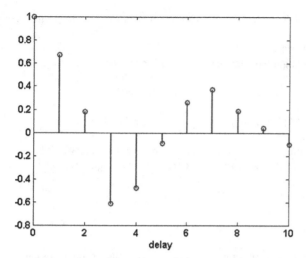

Figure 9-2. *Auto-correlation of the time series data x[n]*

Regression

For such a model, we can run the linear regression to compute the values of *a* and *b* in the following way

```
xprev3=x(1:end-3);
xprev1=x(3:end-1);
xcurrent=x(4:end);
A= [xprev1 xprev3]\xcurrent;
a=A(1);
b=A(2);
```

Forecasting

Based on the proposed model, we can now predict the future values for the time series. For example, tomorrow's rainfall can be predicted (one step prediction) as

```
xprev3ext=x(1:end-2);
xprev1ext=x(3:end);
xtomorrow=a*xprev3ext(end)+b*xprev1ext(end);
xcurrentext=[xcurrent;xtomorrow];
```

Further data can be forcasted by iterating the above one step prediction multiple times. For example, 10 samples of the future data can be predicted as

```
for i=1:10
                    xprev3ext=x(1:end-2);
                    xprev1ext=x(3:end);
                    xtomorrow=a*xprev3ext(end)+b*xprev1ext(end);
                    xcurrentext=[xcurrent;xtomorrow];
                    x=[x;xtomorrow];
end
```

Neural Networks

In previous sections, we have learnt how we can fit a general linear or nonlinear model for a given data set. These kinds of models work well when the data follows such a relation, at least approximately. However, real systems are very complex and such a simple relation is often not able to accurately model the dynamics behind the data. In such cases, when we know nothing about the relation between covariates and response variable, we can still model the data using artificial neural networks.

A neural network tries to imitate the biological neural system (brain) to learn the relation. The covariates act as input to such a network and the value of the response variable is the target output. A neural network consists of many neurons organized in multiple layers. In any layers, each neuron takes output responses from the previous layers, combines them with some weights, generates a response (according to some input-output relation known as the activation function) and feeds it to the neurons of the next layer. In other words, if the response of the previous layer of neurons is denoted by the vector u, the neuron j will first compute a linear combination v of the elements of the vector u using the weights and biases stored in that neuron

$$v_j = \sum w_{ij} v_i + b_j,$$

then computes its response as

$$u_j' = f(v_j)$$

and passes u_j' to the next layer. The first layer takes input from the given data set and is known as the input layer. The last layer which generates the final output of the neural network is known as the output layer. Interior layers which pass responses from the input to the output layers through them are called hidden layers. The number of hidden layers and neurons in each layer define the degree of freedom available in a particular instance of a neural network and should be set according to the complexity of the data we want to fit the model to.

A network is initialized with some weights and biases and it then adjusts its weights and biases to match its output to the target outputs (this process is known as learning or training). There are multiple types of models and training algorithms available in literature. We can also implement such algorithms by scratch, however in this section, we will concentrate on implementation using MATLAB's inbuilt functions. All these methods are bundled together in the MATLAB Neural Network Toolbox.

Feedforward Networks

Let us consider a system that has three inputs a, b and c and an output y. We collect the values of inputs and output at some fixed time interval to get the data matrices A, B, C and Y respectively. Generally, we don't know anything about the relation between the inputs and output. However, for data generation purposes only, assume that the following relation

$$y = 5a + bc + 7c$$

exists between the inputs and output with some amount of measurement error. The following lines of code generate data for our example. Note that this is not part of neural network fitting as the data should come from experiments or acquisition.

```
a= rand(1,1000);
b=rand(1,1000);
c=rand(1,1000);
n=rand(1,1000)*0.05;
y=a*5+b.*c+7*c+n;
```

Here n is the noise which accounts for measurement and system errors. We added this deliberately to make the data look more like a real data. The matrices representing the inputs and target output for the neural network can be defined as

```
I=[a; b; c];
O=y;
```

Here each column represents a covariate and each row represent a sample of the data obtained from an experiment.

We will construct a feedforward neural network with one input and one output layer. The number of neurons in the input layer is taken as 5. Since we have only one output, the output layer must have only one neuron. We will use MATLAB's inbuilt function newff to construct the initial untrained model. The function newff requires the following three inputs:

R: R is a two column matrix defining the range of data. Each row in any column refers to one covariate. The first column represents the minimum possible value of all the covariates and the second row represents the maximum possible value of the covariates.

S: S contains the size of each layer.

Type: Type is a cell matrix containing the activation method for neurons in each layer.

Since all three inputs range from 0 to 1 in the example, R is defined as follows

```
R=[0 1; 0 1 ; 0 1];
```

S will be

```
S=[5 1];
```

We take the activation for the first neuron layer as tansig and the second as purelin.

```
type={'tansig','purelin'};
```

Now we can call the newff function in the following way to generate the initial model

```
net = newff(R,S,type);
```

The second step is to train the neural network so that it can adjust its weights to match the output to the desired output values. We can use the train function which requires model, input data and target values as its input.

```
net=train(net,I,O);
```

MATLAB displays the mean square error as the network gets trained (see Figure 9-3) and outputs the trained network with optimal weights which can now be used to predict output for new input values. To evaluate the performance of the trained model, we will pass the original inputs to it and compare the predicted output to the target output values using the scatter plot in the following way (see Figure 9-4).

```
O1=sim(net,I);
plot(1:1000,O,1:1000,O1);
scatter(O,O1);
```

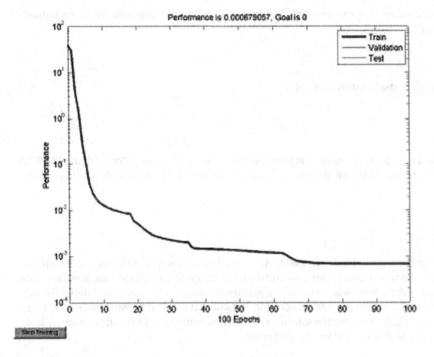

Figure 9-3. *Training errors in a neural network fitting*

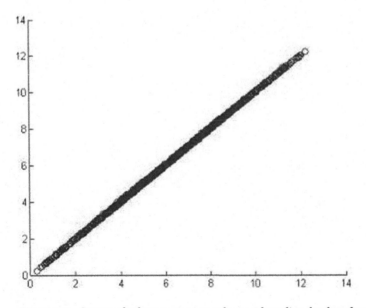

Figure 9-4. *Scatter plot between target values and predicted values from the trained neural network*

The trained model contains the values of optimal weights and biases. To access the weight matrix of the trained model, we use the following syntax

```
disp(net.IW{1});
```

which displays the values of weights for the input layer. Similarly

```
disp(net.LW{2,1})
```

displays the layer weights.

There are many types of neural networks and training algorithms. Interested readers are referred to the MATLAB documentation on neural networks online. MATLAB also provides a GUI tool nntool which helps us to model, train and simulate interactively.

Summary

In this chapter, we learned the basic concepts behind regression. We learned various ways to fit linear and nonlinear models for any given data. We then discussed time series data and a simplistic approach to modeling this data using autoregressive models and predicting the future values. Finally, we learned the concept behind neural networks and modeling through neural networks with the help of a simple example. We saw that a neural network can model very complex and nonlinear relations accurately, however the selection of an optimal number of neurons and layers and appropriate activation functions must be determined by trial and error.

CHAPTER 10

■ ■ ■

Differential Equations and System Dynamics

In Chapter 5, we saw how we can simulate a continuous process given by the update equations which define the rate of change of the process in terms of the current and previous values of the process. A real world system is a combination of interdependent processes which may be hidden or visible to the outside world. A mathematical model of the system generally consists of the update equations (known as state equations) of all such processes and these processes themselves determine the system dynamics. As discussed earlier, the update equations of the continuous time processes are in the form of differential equations. In this chapter, we will first learn to solve differential equations to compute their behavior at different time samples. Using the previous tools and the tools developed in this chapter, we will then learn to simulate the system dynamics of a system to visualize its dynamics and outputs with varying time.

Differential Equations

A differential equation defines the derivatives of one or more variables as a function of themselves. Finding the expressions of these variables in terms of the independent variables is known as solving the differential equation. As we will see later, differential equations play a major role in engineering applications due to their capability to model system dynamics. There are two major types of differential equations: ordinary differential equations and partial differential equations.

Ordinary Differential Equations

Ordinary Differential Equations (ODEs) are differential equations with only one independent variable of the following form

$$\frac{dy}{dx} = f(y, x)$$

where x is the independent variable. To obtain a particular solution to these equations, some further conditions must be defined. Depending on the type of conditions defined, ODEs can be further classified as IVPs (Initial Value Problems) and BVPs (Boundary Value Problems).

Initial Value Problems

If the values of all dependent variables or their derivatives are given at some initial point $x=x_0$, the problem is known as an initial value problem. An IVP can be easily solved using MATLAB's inbuilt functions. However, we will first implement our own simplistic method to solve a differential equation, which will help us to understand the basic functioning behind the inbuilt functions. Then we will see how we can solve the same problem using inbuilt functions from MATLAB. The first step before we can solve an ODE in MATLAB is to convert it to a set of first order equations.

Consider the following differential equation in t

$$\frac{d^2x}{dt^2} + 2\left(\frac{dx}{dt}\right) + 4x = 0$$

with the initial values given as

$$x(t=0)=1 \ and \ x'(t=0)=0.5;$$

To convert this ODE to a set of first order differential equations, we need to define two variables y_1 and y_2. The number of variables needed is dependent on (and generally equal to) the order of the original differential equation. Now assume that $y_1 = x$ & $y_2 = \frac{dy_1}{dt}$. Therefore the original equation can be represented as

$$\frac{dy_2}{dt} = -2y_2 - 4y_1$$

with

$$\frac{dy_1}{dt} = y_2.$$

Similarly the initial conditions will be transformed as $y_1 (t=0) = 1$ and $y_2 (t=0) = 0.5$.
We will now use the matrix representation

$$\mathbf{y} = \begin{bmatrix} \mathbf{y}_1 \\ \mathbf{y}_2 \end{bmatrix}, \dot{\mathbf{y}} = \begin{bmatrix} \dot{\mathbf{y}}_1 \\ \dot{\mathbf{y}}_2 \end{bmatrix}$$

to denote the set of variables y_1 and y_2 and the set of their derivatives. With such a representation, we can denote the set of first order differential equations as

$$\dot{\mathbf{y}} = f(\mathbf{y},t)$$

where $f: R^2 \times R \rightarrow R^2$ is the function relating derivatives to variables.

A Simplistic Method

Now we will follow steps similar to those described in Chapter 5 to simulate the process $y(t)$. Take a time step δt. At any time t, the value of $y_1(t+\delta t)$ and $y_2(t+\delta t)$ at the next time step is given as

$$y_1(t+\delta t) = y_1(t) + \delta t \frac{dy_1}{dt} = y_2(t) + \delta t(y_2)$$

$$y_2(t+\delta t) = y_2(t) + \delta t \frac{dy_2}{dt} = y_2(t) + \delta t(-2y_2 - 4y_1)$$

This update step can be implemented by the following code

```
y_diff(1,:)=y(2);
y_diff(2,:)=y(1)*4-2*y(2);
ynew=y+y_diff*deltat;
```

Now we need to repeat the update step for the desired time duration, with the initial values $y_0 = \begin{bmatrix} 1 \\ 0.05 \end{bmatrix}$ as given to us by the initial conditions. The following code implements our method and plots the response $\mathbf{y}(t)$ (see Figure 10-1). The solid line curve denotes the response $x(t)$.

```
y_0=[1;.05];
deltat=0.01;
t=0:deltat:10;
y=y_0;
yt=zeros(2,length(t));
for i=1:length(t)
        y_diff(1,:)=y(2);
        y_diff(2,:)=y(1)*4-2*y(2);
        ynew=y+y_diff*deltat;
        yt(:,i)= ynew;
        y=ynew;
end
plot(t,yt);
```

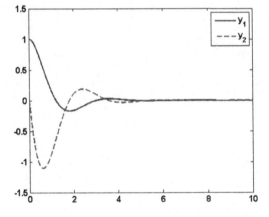

Figure 10-1. *Simulated response of y(t)*

Inbuilt functions

Now let us see how we can solve the same problem using MATLAB's inbuilt functions. Since there are multiple algorithms to solve an ODE depending on its characteristics, MATLAB provides many inbuilt functions. However, all of these inbuilt functions have a similar syntax. We will use one such inbuilt function, ode45, to solve our example problem.

To use ode45, we first need to define a MATLAB function that takes x and t as input, outputs $\dot{x}$ and implements $f\colon R \times R^2 \to R^2$.

```
function dydt=funcdiff(t,y)
dydt(1,:)=y(2);
dydt(2,:)=-y(1)*4-2*y(2);
```

Let us first discuss the syntax of ode45. The function ode45 expects the following inputs:

- *Function handle*: a handle for the function which implements $f\colon R \times R^2 \to R^2$ to compute derivatives of **y** at given **y** and t

- *Time span*: the desired time duration for which we want to simulate the process

- *Initial values*: the initial values of the vector **y**

- *Options*: an option structure to specify solver configurations and preferences which can be set by odeset

Now in a separate scriptfile or function file, we will write the code to define the relevant variables and inputs, call ode45, and plot the results (see Figure 10-2).

```
tspan=[0 10];
y0=[1;0.05];
[t y]=ode45(@funcdiff,tspan,y0);
plot(t,y);
```

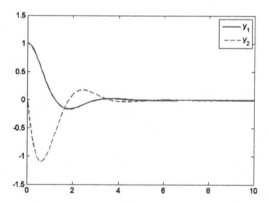

Figure 10-2. *Solution of the ODE using ode45*

Based on different requirements and characteristics of the ODEs, we need to use different solvers. Table 10-1 lists the inbuilt MATLAB functions and corresponding solvers. For ODEs the calling syntax is the same for all solvers except for ode15i.

Table 10-1. *ODE solvers and inbuilt functions in MATLAB*

Solver	Type of problem	Method
ode45	Nonstiff differential equations	Runge-Kutta
ode23	Nonstiff differential equations	Runge-Kutta
ode113	Nonstiff differential equations	Adams
ode15s	Stiff differential equations and DAEs	NDFs (BDFs)
ode23s	Stiff differential equations	Rosenbrock
ode23t	Moderately stiff differential equations and DAEs	Trapezoidal rule
ode23tb	Stiff differential equations	TR-BDF2
ode15i	Fully implicit differential equations	BDFs

Note that some methods have 's' at the end to denote that they can solve ODEs which are stiff. A stiff ODE is an ODE where the derivatives of the variables vary with time by orders of magnitude. How to determine whether the problem is stiff or not is sometimes guesswork. In practice, we should try ode45 first for any problem. If it fails or is very inefficient (e.g. it takes too much time to finish) and we suspect that the problem is stiff, we should switch to ode15s. Also, ode15s is suited for differential-algebraic problems.

Events

If at any point of time during the simulation of an ODE the current values of the variables satisfy some particular condition $g(\mathbf{y}(t)) = 0$, we say that an event has occurred. The condition can be a simple comparison of variables such as $y_1 = y_2$ or the detection of an overflow such as $y_1 = -\epsilon$. The detection of events may help us in deciding the correctness of the solution or termination conditions. Sometimes an event can reset the value of a variable, such as the change of a ball's velocity when it collides with the floor. MATLAB provides an option in its inbuilt functions to detect an event while solving an ODE.

To use this detection feature, the first step is to create an event detection function (say 'eventsfunc') with the following syntax:

```
function [value,isterminal,direction] = eventsfunc(t,y)
```

This function should return three outputs:

- *value*: Output value denotes the LHS of the condition $g(\mathbf{y}) = 0$ at input $\mathbf{y}$ and t. The occurrence of the event should be equivalent to this value becoming zero. If we need to detect multiple types of events, the value should be a vector with each value denoting an event condition.

- *isterminal*: Output isterminal specifies whether the program should terminate if an event condition is met. The size of isterminal should be the same as value in case of the detection of multiple events. Use 1 to specify termination and 0 for continuation.

- *direction*: Output direction specifies if an event should be detected for all zero crossings of $g(\mathbf{y})$ or only for positive or negative crossings. Use 0 to specify all zero crossings, 1 for positive zero crossings and -1 for negative zero crossings.

Consider the case where we have to detect all the events where $y_1(t) = y_2(t)$ in the decreasing direction and we need to terminate the ODE simulation if the event occurs. Here $g(\mathbf{y}) = y_1 - y_2$. The event detection function should look like the following:

```
function [value,isterminal,direction] = eventsfunc_1(t,y)
        value = y(1)-y(2);  % Detect y(1)-y(2)=0
        isterminal = 1;
        direction = -1;
```

The second step is to set the Events options in the output structure with the eventsfunc_1 function handle using the odeset function.

```
options=odeset('Events',@eventsfunc_1);
```

Now we can rerun ode45 with this option structure to enable the detection of events. We need to use the following syntax to collect all events that have occurred:

```
[t y timeevents ye indexe]=ode45(@funcdiff,tspan,y0,options);
```

Boundary Value Problems

A boundary condition specifies values of variables at the boundaries of the region of interest. A BVP is an ODE with some boundary conditions on the dependent variables or their derivatives. For example, consider the following ODE

$$\frac{dx}{dt} = f(x,t)$$

for $a \le t \le b$. The values of the dependent variable at the boundary are $x(a)$ & $x(b)$. The boundary condition can be given in the form $g(y(a), y(b)) = 0$. The MATLAB inbuilt function bvp4c is used to solve this type of problem.

Let us consider the following BVP problem. Solve

$$x'' + \frac{t}{6}x' + x = 0$$

for $0 \le t \le 1$ with boundary conditions $x'(0) = 0$ & $x(1) = 1$. Similarly to our treatment of the IVP, let us first convert this ODE to a set of first order differential equations. Define $y_1 = x$ and $y_2 = y_1'$. Now the given ODE can be written as

$$y_2' = -\frac{x}{6}y_2 - y_1.$$

Let us define the function $\dot{\mathbf{y}} = f(\mathbf{y},t)$ where $\mathbf{y} = \begin{bmatrix} y_1 \\ y_2 \end{bmatrix}$, using the primary function fun_bvpode

```
function dydx = fun_bvpode(x,y)
        dydx = [y(2); -x/6*y(2)-y(1) ];
```

Since the boundary here is $a = 0$ and $b = 1$, we need the values of y_1 and y_2 at 0 and 1. Let us denote the value of the vector $\mathbf{y}$ at a as $\mathbf{ya}$ and at b as $\mathbf{yb}$. To specify the boundary, we need to define a function (boundary conditions) which takes the current values of $\mathbf{ya}$ and $\mathbf{yb}$ as input and computes the residual difference between the desired boundary values and the current values.

```
function res = boundary_conditions(ya,yb)
        res = [ ya(2);yb(1)-1 ];
```

Note that unlike IVPs, there are no initial conditions specified in BVPs. Therefore we need to take an initial guess to start the simulation. Suppose we take the initial values at each point to be constant and the same as the boundary. Hence $y_1(t)=1$ and $y_2(t)=0$ for all t. MATLAB provides an inbuilt function bvpinit to help us create the required structure for the initial guess. The function bvpinit requires two matrices: a mesh of the independent variable t and an initial guess of the value of the dependent variables at each point of this mesh. Since we have chosen a constant value as a guess, we can just supply these constant values. If we had chosen to specify an initial guess which varies across t, we would need to pass a Y matrix with size equal to the size of the t mesh. We can also choose to give a function handle to bvpinit which can calculate the y from t. For this example, let us stick to the constant initial guess.

```
guess = [1;0];
solinit = bvpinit(linspace(0,1,1500),guess);
```

Now we can call the BVP solver bvp4c to solve the above problem with the derivative function, boundary condition function and the initial guess of the solution as inputs.

```
Sol=bvp4c(@fun_bvpode,@boundary_conditions,solinit);
```

The output Sol is a structure with the field x containing the mesh of independent variables and the field y with corresponding y values. The solution can be plotted by the following code (see Figure 10-3).

```
plot(Sol.x,Sol.y,'LineWidth',2);
```

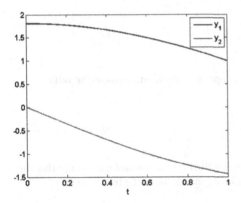

Figure 10-3. *Solution of the BVP using bvp4c*

Partial Differential Equations

Partial differential equations are differential equation involving multiple independent variables and partial derivatives of the dependent variables. MATLAB provides the inbuilt pdepe partial differential equation solver to solve any system of parabolic and elliptic PDEs which can be written in the form

$$c(x,t,u,u_x)u_t = x^{-m}\frac{\partial}{\partial x}\left(x^m f(x,t,u,u_x)\right)+s(x,t,u,u_x)$$

with initial conditions $u(x,t_0) = u_0(x)$ and boundary conditions of the form $p(x,t,u) + q(x,t)f(x,t,u,u_x) = 0$ at $x = x_1$ & $x = x_u$. Here c,f,s,p,u and q are some functions with appropriate inputs.

We will start with a standard example taken from the MATLAB documentation on pdepe. Let us consider the following differential equation with t and x as independent variables and $u(x,t)$ as the dependent variable

$$\pi^2 \frac{\partial u}{\partial t} = \frac{\partial^2 u}{\partial x^2}$$

for $0 \le x \le 1$ with initial condition $u(x,0) = \sin(\pi x)$ and boundary condition $u(0,t) = 0$ & $\pi e^{-t} + u_x(1,t) = 0$.

First we have to convert these equations to standard format to get the functions c, s, f, p and q, which may be done by direct comparison. Note that we can rewrite the original differential equation as

$$\pi^2 \frac{\partial u}{dt} = x^0 \frac{\partial}{\partial x}\left(x^0 \frac{\partial u}{\partial x} \right) + 0$$

and by direct comparison we can see that

$$m = 0$$
$$c(x,t,u,u_x) = \pi^2$$
$$f(x,t,u,u_x) = u_x$$
$$s(x,t,u,u_x) = 0$$

Now we must define a MATLAB function which should accept x, t, u and u_x as input and output the value of c, f and s.

```
function [c f s] = funcpde(x,t,u,ux)
c=pi^2;
f=ux;
s=0;
```

For the initial conditions, we must define an initial function which accepts x as input and outputs the value of $u(0,x)$

```
function u=funcinit(x)
u=sin(pi*x);
```

Now before we can define the boundary conditions, we need to compute the functions p and q by comparing the given boundary conditions with the standard form. We see that the boundary conditions can be rewritten as

$$\pi e^{-t} + 1 \cdot f\left(x,t,u,u_x\right)_{at\, x=1} = 0$$
$$u(x,t) + 0 \cdot f\left(x,t,u,u_x\right)_{at\, x=0} = 0$$

We can see that $p(x,t,u) = \pi e^{-t}$, $q(x,t) = 1$ at $x = 1$ and $p(x,t,u) = u(x,t)$, $q(x,t) = 0$ at $x = 0$. To specify the boundary conditions, we must define a function that accepts the lower and upper limits of x (x_l and x_r), the value of u at x_l and x_r (respectively u_l and u_r) and t as input and outputs the value of p and q at x_l and x_r.

```
function [pl ql pr qr]=funcbv(xl,ul,xr,ur,t)
pl=ul;ql=0;
pr=pi*exp(-t);qr=1;
```

As a final step, in a separate script/function file, we need to specify the x and t meshgrid on which the computations must be performed. The accuracy of the solution will depend on the grid.

```
X=[0:.05:1];T=[0:.1:5];
```

Now, after defining all the required functions and variables, we can call the pdepe solver. Let us first understand the general syntax of pdepe given as

```
sol = pdepe(m,pdefun,icfun,bcfun,xmesh,tspan);
```

where it expects following inputs:

m	Order of symmetry *m*
pdefun	Handle of the function representing the differential equation
icfun	Handle of the function defining initial conditions
bcfun	Handle of the function defining boundary conditions
xmesh	Sample points for X
tspan	Time samples

and outputs a three-dimensional array with the first dimension representing time, the second dimension representing xmesh points and the third dimension representing different components of *u* if *u* is a multidimensional function.

Therefore, we can call the pdepe following the above syntax

```
m=0;
sol=pdepe(m,@funcpde,@funcinit,@funcbv,X,T);
```

The output from the pdepe solver can be visualized using the surf function using the following code (see Figure 10-4).

```
[Xm Ym]=meshgrid(X,T);
surf(Xm,Ym,sol(:,:,1));
```

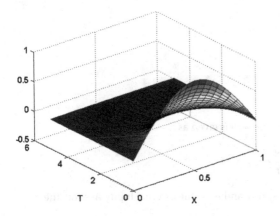

Figure 10-4. *Surface plot of u(t,x)*

System Dynamics

In this section, we will see how we can simulate a linear time-invariant (LTI) system dynamics to see the response of its output, using what we have learnt in the previous sections. A typical LTI system with input $u(t)$ and output $y(t)$ can be modeled by the following equations

$$\dot{x}(t) = Ax + Bu(t)$$
$$y(t) = Cx(t) + Du(t)$$

where $\mathbf{x}(t)$ is a vector consisting of internal variables of the system, known as state variables. The above equations are therefore called state equations and such a model is called a state space model. Let us first see an example of a real world system. Consider a system comprising a block attached to a wall via a spring (see Figure 10-5) where we are interested in computing the variation $x(t)$ of the location of the block with time.

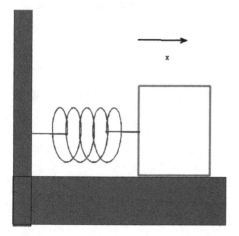

Figure 10-5. *A spring-box system*

The forces applied on the block when it is at a distance x from the wall is given as

$$F = -kx - b\frac{dx}{dt} + F_{ext}$$

where k is the spring constant, b is the damping coefficient of the spring and F_{ext} is the external input. Assume the mass of the block is m, then the force equation can be written as

$$ma = -kx - b\frac{dx}{dt} + F_{ext}$$

$$m\frac{d^2x}{dt^2} = -kx - b\frac{dx}{dt} + F_{ext}$$

which is an ODE representing the system's dynamics. Let us convert it to a set of first order differential equations. Take the following two variables x and $v = \dfrac{dx}{dt}$. With the help of these variables, the ODE can be written as

$$m\frac{dv}{dt} = -kx - bv + F_{ext}.$$

Therefore the system dynamics can be modeled by the following two equations

$$\frac{dv}{dt} = -\frac{b}{m}v - \frac{k}{m}x + \frac{1}{m}F_{ext}$$

$$\frac{dx}{dt} = v$$

Using the matrix representation $z(t) = \begin{bmatrix} v(t) \\ x(t) \end{bmatrix}$, we can write the above set of equations as

$$\begin{bmatrix} v \\ x \end{bmatrix} = \frac{d}{dt}\begin{bmatrix} v \\ x \end{bmatrix} = \begin{bmatrix} -\frac{b}{m} & -\frac{k}{M} \\ 1 & 0 \end{bmatrix} \times \begin{bmatrix} v \\ x \end{bmatrix} + \begin{bmatrix} \frac{1}{m} \\ 0 \end{bmatrix} \times F$$

Since the desired output $y(t)$ is in fact $x(t)$, it can be rewritten in terms of the vector $z(t)$ as

$$y = \begin{bmatrix} 0 & 1 \end{bmatrix}z + \begin{bmatrix} 0 \end{bmatrix}F$$

Comparing these equations with the standard equations of a state space model, we get

$$A = \begin{bmatrix} -\frac{b}{m} & -\frac{k}{m} \\ 1 & 0 \end{bmatrix} \times \begin{bmatrix} v \\ x \end{bmatrix}, B = \begin{bmatrix} \frac{1}{m} \\ 0 \end{bmatrix}$$

$$C = \begin{bmatrix} 0 & 1 \end{bmatrix}, \quad D = 0.$$

Here v and x are the state variables of the spring-box system.

Simulation of the System

Since the system dynamics is represented in the form of an ODE, it can be easily simulated by solving the ODE. Let us assume the initial condition is given as

$$x(t=0) = L, v(t=0) = 0.$$

and the external input is given as

$$F = 0.9\sin 2w_b t.$$

Let us first define the dynamics function in a separate function file

```
function dzdt=funcsysdym(t,z)
m=100;
b=2.0;
k=20.0;w_b=10;
A=[-b/m -k/m;1 0];B=[1/m;0];
C=[0 1]; D=0;
F=0.9*sin(2*w_b*t);
dzdt=A*z+B*F;
```

Now we should define the initial conditions in a separate script file and call the ode45 solver, plotting the result (see Figure 10-6).

```
Tspan=[0:10];
L=10;
yo=[0;L];
[t y]=ode45(@funcsysdym,tspan,yo);
plot(t,y);
```

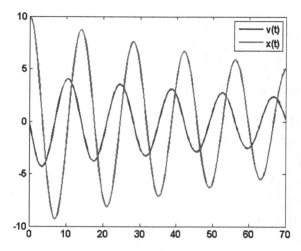

Figure 10-6. *Response of the sping-box system for an external force* F_{Ext}

Step Response

If the external output is a step input, the system response is known as a step response. We can easily compute the step response by running ode45 with the following modified dynamics function (see Figure 10-7):

```
function dzdt=funcsysdym(t,z)
m=100;
b=10;
k=20;
A=[-b/m -k/m;1 0];B=[1/m;0];
C=[0 1]; D=0;
F=50*(t>=0);
dzdt=A*z+B*F;
```

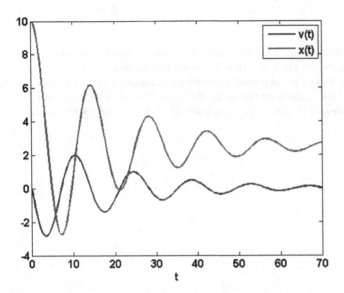

Figure 10-7. *Step response of the spring-box system*

Another way to compute the response is by using MATLAB's Control Toolbox. First we need to make a state space model object from the matrices *A,B,C* and *D* using the ss function.

```
A=[-b/m -k/m;1 0];B=[1/m;0];
C=[0 1]; D=0;
Sys1=ss(A,B,C,D);
```

Now we can simulate the system using the step function for an arbitrary time duration Trange

```
Trange=10;
[y t]=step(Sys1,Trange)
```

which gives us the t matrix containing the time samples and corresponding output values y which can be plotted to view the response.

```
plot(t,y);
```

We can also simulate the system for an arbitrary input signal using the lsim function. We first need to define the input signal as a time signal pair vector in the following way

```
tr=0:.01:1;
w_b=10;F=0.1*sin(2*w_b*tr);
```

and then we can call lsim and plot the response outputs.

```
[y t]=lmsim(Sys1,tr,F);
plot(t,y);
```

Summary

In this chapter, we have learnt how we can numerically solve any ODE with initial or boundary conditions using MATLAB's inbuilt functions. We have also learnt how we can implement a solution method for an initial value problem from scratch. Then we considered parabolic and elliptical partial differential equations and learnt how to numerically solve such equations. In the latter half of the chapter, we discussed the relation between linear system dynamics and ODEs and learned how we can simulate an LTI system response using MATLAB's inbuilt ODE solvers and Control Toolbox functions.

Index

Get the eBook for only $10!

> Now you can take the weightless companion with you anywhere, anytime. Your purchase of this book entitles you to 3 electronic versions for only $10.

This Apress title will prove so indispensible that you'll want to carry it with you everywhere, which is why we are offering the eBook in 3 formats for only $10 if you have already purchased the print book.

Convenient and fully searchable, the PDF version enables you to easily find and copy code—or perform examples by quickly toggling between instructions and applications. The MOBI format is ideal for your Kindle, while the ePUB can be utilized on a variety of mobile devices.

Go to www.apress.com/promo/tendollars to purchase your companion eBook.

Apress®
THE EXPERT'S VOICE™